PROFESSOR JOHN RUSKIN, M.A.

True and

Beautiful

❧

JOHN RUSKIN

Fredonia Books
Amsterdam, The Netherlands

True and Beautiful:
Painting, Morals and Religion

by
John Ruskin

ISBN: 1-58963-936-7

Copyright © 2002 by Fredonia Books

Reprinted from the 1886 edition

Fredonia Books
Amsterdam, The Netherlands
http://www.fredoniabooks.com

CONTENTS.

PAINTING.

POETRY.

MORALS AND RELIGION.

PAINTING.

———◆———

Painting, with all its technicalities, difficulties, and particu lar ends, is nothing but a noble and expressive language, in valuable as the vehicle of thought, but by itself nothing.

THE

TRUE AND THE BEAUTIFUL

IN

Nature, Art, Morals, and Religion.

PAINTING.

CHARACTERISTICS OF "GREATNESS OF STYLE" IN PAINTING.

I. CHOICE OF NOBLE SUBJECT.—Greatness of style consists then: first, in the habitual choice of subjects of thought which involve wide interests and profound passions, as opposed to those which involve narrow interests and slight passions. The style is greater or less in exact proportion to the nobleness of the interests and passions involved in the subject. The habitual choice of sacred subjects, such as the Nativity, Transfiguration, Crucifixion (if the choice be sincere),

3

implies that the painter has a natural disposition to dwell on the highest thoughts of which humanity is capable; it constitutes him so far forth a painter of the highest order, as, for instance, Leonardo, in his painting of the Last Supper: he who delights in representing the acts or meditations of great men, as, for instance, Raphael painting the School of Athens, is, so far forth, a painter of the second order: he who represents the passions and events of ordinary life, of the third. And in this ordinary life, he who represents deep thoughts and sorrows, as, for instance, Hunt, in his Claudio and Isabella, and such other works, is of the highest rank in his sphere; and he who represents the slight malignities and passions of the drawing-room, as, for instance, Leslie, of the second rank: he who represents the sports of boys or simplicities of clowns, as Webster or Teniers, of the third rank; and he who represents brutalities and vices (for delight in them, and not for rebuke of them), of no rank at all, or rather of a negative rank, holding a certain order in the abyss.

The reader will, I hope, understand how much importance is to be attached to the sentence in the first parenthesis, " if the choice be sincere;" for choice of subject is, of course, only available as a criterion of the rank of the painter, when it is made from the heart. Indeed, in the lower orders of painting, the choice is always made from such heart as the painter has; for his selection of the brawls of peasants or sports of children can, of course, proceed only from the fact that he has more sympathy with such brawls or pastimes than with nobler subjects. But the choice of the higher kind of subjects is often insincere; and may, therefore, afford no real criterion of the painter's rank.

It must be remembered, that in nearly all the great periods of art the choice of subject has not been left to the painter. His employer,—abbot, baron, or monarch,—determined for him whether he should earn his bread by making cloisters bright with choirs of saints, painting coats of arms on leaves of romances, or decorating presence-chambers with complimentary mythology; and his own personal feelings are ascertainable only by watching, in the themes assigned to him, what are the points in which he seems to take most pleasure.

II. LOVE OF BEAUTY.—The second characteristic of the great school of art is, that it introduces in the conception of its subject as much beauty as is possible, consistently with truth.*

---

* As here, for the first time, I am obliged to use the terms Truth and Beauty in a kind of opposition, I must therefore stop for a moment to state clearly the relation of these two qualities of art; and to protest against the

For instance, in any subject consisting of a number of figures, it will make as many of those figures beautiful as the faithful representation of

---

vulgar and foolish habit of confusing truth and beauty with each other.   People with shallow powers of thought, desiring to flatter themselves with the sensation of having attained profundity, are continually doing the most serious mischief by introducing confusion into plain matters, and then valuing themselves on being confounded.   Nothing is more common than to hear people who desire to be thought philosophical, declare that "beauty is truth" and "truth is beauty."   I would most earnestly beg every sensible person who hears such an assertion made, to nip the germinating philosopher in his ambiguous bud; and beg him, if he really believes his own assertion, never thenceforward to use two words for the same thing.   The fact is, truth and beauty are entirely distinct, though often related things.   One is a property of statements, the other of objects.   The statement that "two and two make four" is true, but it is neither beautiful nor ugly, for it is invisible; a rose is lovely, but it is neither true nor false, for it is silent.   That which shows nothing cannot be fair, and that which asserts nothing cannot be false.   Even the ordinary use of the words false and true as applied to artificial and real things, is inaccurate.   An artificial rose is not a "false" rose, it is not a rose at all.   The falseness is in the person who states, or induces the belief, that it *is* a rose.

Now, therefore, in things concerning art, the words true and false are only to be rightly used, while the picture is considered as a statements of facts.   The painter asserts that this which he has painted is the form of a dog, a man, or a tree.   If it be *not* the form of a dog, a man,

humanity will admit. It will not deny the facts of ugliness or decrepitude, or relative inferiority and superiority of feature as necessarily mani-

---

or a tree, the painter's statement is false; and therefore we justly speak of a false line, or false color; not that any line or color can in themselves be false, but they become so when they convey a statement that they resemble something which they do *not* resemble. But the beauty of the lines or colors is wholly independent of any such statement. They may be beautiful lines, though quite inaccurate, and ugly lines though quite faithful. A picture may be frightfully ugly, which represents with fidelity some base circumstance of daily life; and a painted window may be exquisitely beautiful, which represents men with eagles' faces, and dogs with blue heads and crimson tails (though by the way, this is not in the strict sense *false* art, as we shall see hereafter, inasmuch as it means no assertion that men ever *had* eagles' faces). If this were not so, it would be inpossible to sacrifice truth to beauty; for to attain the one would always be to attain the other. But, unfortunately, this sacrifice is exceedingly possible, and it is chiefly this which characterises the false schools of high art, so far as high art consists in the pursuit of beauty. For although truth and beauty are independent of each other, it does not follow that we are at liberty to pursue whichever we please. They are indeed separable, but it is wrong to separate them; they are to be sought together in the order of their worthiness: that is to say, truth first, and beauty afterwards. High art differs from low art in possessing an excess of beauty in addition to its truth, not in possessing an excess of beauty inconsistent with truth.

fested in a crowd, but it will, so far as it is in its
power, seek for and dwell upon the fairest forms,
and in all things insist on the beauty that is in
them, not on the ugliness. In this respect,
schools of art become higher in exact proportion
to the degree in which they apprehend and love
the beautiful. Thus, Angelico, intensely loving
all spiritual beauty, will be of the highest rank;
and Paul Veronese and Correggio, intensely loving physical and corporeal beauty, of the second
rank; and Albert Durer, Rubens, and in general
the Northern artists apparently insensible to
beauty, and caring only for truth, whether
shapely or not, of the third rank; and Teniers
and Salvator, Caravaggio, and other such wor-
shippers of the depraved, of no rank, or, as we
said before, of a certain order in the abyss.

The corruption of the schools of high art, so
far as this particular quality is concerned, consists in the sacrifice of truth to beauty. Great
art dwells on all that is beautiful; but false art
omits or changes all that is ugly. Great art accepts Nature as she is, but directs the eyes and
thoughts to what is most perfect in her; false art
saves itself the trouble of direction by removing
or altering whatever it thinks objectionable.
The evil results of which proceeding are twofold.

First. That beauty deprived of its proper foils

and adjuncts ceases to be enjoyed as beauty, just as light deprived of all shadow ceases to be enjoyed as light. A white canvas cannot produce an effect of sunshine; the painter must darken it in some places before he can make it look luminous in others; nor can an uninterrupted succession of beauty produce the true effect of beauty; it must be foiled by inferiority before its own power can be developed. Nature has for the most part mingled her inferior and nobler elements as she mingles sunshine with shade, giving due use and influence to both, and the painter who chooses to remove the shadow, perishes in the burning desert he has created. The truly high and beautiful art of Angelico is continually refreshed and strengthened by his frank portraiture of the most ordinary features of his brother monks, and of the recorded peculiarities of ungainly sanctity; but the modern German and Raphaelesque schools lose all honor and nobleness in barber-like admiration of handsome faces, and have, in fact, no real faith except in straight noses and curled hair. Paul Veronese opposes the dwarf to the soldier, and the negress to the queen; Shakspere places Caliban beside Miranda, and Autolycus beside Perdita; but the vulgar idealist withdraws his beauty to the safety of the saloon, and his innocence to the seclusion of the cloister; he pretends that he does this in delicacy of choice and purity of sentiment, while in truth he has neither courage to front the monster, nor wit enough to furnish the knave.

It is only by the habit of representing faithfully all things, that we can truly learn what is beautiful and what is not. The ugliest objects contain some element of beauty; and in all, it is an element peculiar to themselves, which cannot be separated from their ugliness, but must either be enjoyed together with it, or not at all. The more a painter accepts nature as he finds it, the more unexpected beauty he discovers in what he at first despised; but once let him arrogate the right of rejection, and he will gradually contract his circle of enjoyment, until what he supposed to be nobleness of selection ends in narrowness of perception. Dwelling perpetually upon one class of ideas, his art becomes at once monstrous and morbid; until at last he cannot faithfully represent even what he chooses to retain; his discrimination contracts into darkness, and his fastidiousness fades into fatuity.

High art, therefore, consists neither in altering, nor in improving nature; but in seeking throughout nature for "whatsoever things are lovely, and whatsoever things are pure;" in loving these, in displaying to the utmost of the painter's power such loveliness as is in them, and directing the thoughts of others to them by winning art, or gentle emphasis. Of the degree in which this can be done, and in which it may be permitted to gather together, without falsifying, the finest forms or thoughts, so as to create a sort of perfect vision, we shall have to speak hereafter: at present, it is enough to remember that art (*cæteris paribus*) is great in exact proportion to the love of beauty shown by the painter, provided that love of beauty forfeit no atom of truth.

III. SINCERITY.—The next* characteristic of great art is that it includes the largest possible quantity of Truth in the most perfect possible harmony. If it were possible for art to give all the truths of nature, it ought to do it. But this is not possible. Choice must always be made of some facts which *can* be represented, from among others which must be passed by in silence, or even, in some respects, misrepresented. The inferior artist chooses unimportant and scattered truths; the great artist chooses the most necessary first, and afterwards the most consistent with these, so as to obtain the greatest possible and most harmonious *sum*. For instance Rembrandt always chooses to represent the exact force with which the light on the most illumined

---

* I name them in order of *in*creasing not decreasing importance.

part of an object is opposed to its obscurer portions. In order to obtain this, in most cases, not very important truth, he sacrifices the light and color of five-sixths of his picture; and the expression of every character of objects which depends on tenderness of shape or tint. But he obtains his single truth, and what picturesque and forcible expression is dependent upon it, with magnificent skill and subtlety. Veronese, on the contrary, chooses to represent the great relations of visible things to each other, to the heaven above, and to the earth beneath them. He holds it more important to show how a figure stands relieved from delicate air, or marble wall; how as a red, or purple, or white figure, it separates itself, in clear discernibility, from things not red, nor purple, nor white; how infinite daylight shines round it; how innumerable veils of faint shadow invest it; how its blackness and darkness are, in the excess of their nature, just as limited and local as its intensity of light: all this, I say, he feels to be more important than showing merely the exact *measure* of the spark of sunshine that gleams on a dagger-hilt.

As its greatness depends on the sum of truth, and this sum of truth can always be increased by delicacy of handling, it follows that all great art must have this delicacy to the utmost possible degree. This rule is infallible and inflexible.

All coarse work is the sign of low art. Only, it is to be remembered, that coarseness must be estimated by the distance from the eye; it being necessary to consult this distance, when great, by laying on touches which appear coarse when seen near; but which, so far from being coarse, are, in reality, more delicate in a master's work than the finest close handling, for they involve a calculation of result, and are laid on with a subtlety of sense precisely correspondent to that with which a good archer draws his bow; the spectator seeing in the action nothing but the strain of the strong arm, while there is, in reality in the finger and eye, an ineffably delicate estimate of distance, and touch on the arrow plume. And, indeed, this delicacy is generally quite per ceptible to those who know what the truth is, for strokes by Tintoret or Paul Veronese, which were done in an instant, and look to an ignorant spectator merely like a violent dash of loaded color (and are, as such, imitated by blundering artists), are, in fact, modulated by the brush and finger to that degree of delicacy that no single grain of the color could be taken from the touch without injury; and little golden particles of it, not the size of a gnat's head, have important share and function in the balances of light in a picture perhaps fifty feet long. Nearly *every* other rule applicable to art has some ex-

ception but this. This has absolutely none. All
great art is delicate art, and all coarse art is bad
art. Nay, even to a certain extent, all *bold* art is
bad art; for boldness is not the proper word to
apply to the courage and swiftness of a great
master, based on knowledge, and coupled with
fear and love. There is as much difference between the boldness of the true and the false masters, as there is between the courage of a pure
woman and the shamelessness of a lost one.

IV. INVENTION.—The last characteristic of
great art is that it must be inventive, that is, be
produced by the imagination. In this respect it
must precisely fulfil the definition already given
of poetry; and not only present grounds for noble emotion, but furnish these grounds by *imaginative power.* Hence there is at once a great
bar fixed between the two schools of Lower and
Higher Art. The lower merely copies what is
set before it, whether in portrait, landscape, or
still-life; the higher either entirely imagines its
subject, or arranges the materials presented to it,
so as to manifest the imaginative power in all
the three phases which have been already explained in the second volume.

And this was the truth which was confusedly
present in Reynolds's mind when he spoke, as
above quoted, of the difference between Historical and Poetical Painting. *Every relation of*

the plain facts which the painter saw is proper *historical* painting.*   If those facts are unimportant (as that he saw a gambler quarrel with another gambler, or a sot enjoying himself with another sot), then the history is trivial; if the facts are important (as that he saw such and such a great man look thus, or act thus, at such a time), then the history is noble: in each case perfect truth of narrative being supposed otherwise the whole thing is worthless, being neither history nor poetry, but plain falsehood. And farther, as greater or less elegance and precision are manifested in the relation or painting of the incidents, the merit of the work varies ; so that, what with difference of subject, and what with difference of treatment, historical painting falls or rises in changeful eminence, from Dutch trivialities to a Velasquez portrait, just as historical talking or writing varies in eminence, from an old woman's story-telling up to Herodotus. Besides which, certain operations of the imagination come into play inevitably, here and there, so as to touch the history with some light of poetry, that is, with some light shot forth of the narrator's mind, or brought out by the way he has put the accidents together ; and wherever the imagination has thus had anything to do

---

* Compare my Edinburgh Lectures, lecture iv. (2d edition).

with the matter at all (and it must be somewhat
cold work where it has not), then, the con-
fines of the lower and higher schools touching
each other, the work is colored by both ; but
there is no reason why, therefore, we should in
the least confuse the historical and poetical
characters, any more than that we should confuse blue with crimson, because they may over-
lap each other, and produce purple.

Now, historical or simply narrative art is very
precious in its proper place and way, but it is
never *great* art until the poetical or imaginative
power touches it ; and in proportion to the
stronger manifestation of this power, it becomes
greater and greater, while the highest art is
purely imaginative, all its materials being wrought
into their form by invention ; and it differs,
therefore, from the simple historical painting,
exactly as Wordsworth's stanza, above quoted,
differs from Saussure's plain narrative of the
parallel fact ; and the imaginative painter differs
from the historical painter in the manner that
Wordsworth differs from Saussure.

Farther, imaginative art always *includes* historical art ; so that, strictly speaking, according
to the analogy above used, we meet with the
pure blue, and with the crimson ruling the blue
and changing it into kingly purple, but not with
the pure crimson : for all imagination must deal

with the knowledge it has before accumulated ; it never produces anything but by combination or contemplation. Creation, in the full sense, is impossible to it. And the mode in which the historical faculties are included by it is often quite simple, and easily seen. Thus, in Hunt's great poetical picture of the Light of the World, the whole thought and arrangement of the picture being imaginative, the several details of it are wrought out with simple portraiture; the ivy, the jewels, the creeping plants, and the moonlight being calmly studied or remembered from the things themselves. But of all these special ways in which the invention works with plain facts, we shall have to treat farther afterwards.

And now, finally, since this poetical power includes the historical, if we glance back to the other qualities required in great art, and put all together, we find that the sum of them is simply the sum of all the powers of man. For as (1) the choice of the high subject involves all conditions of right moral choice, and as (2) the love of beauty involves all conditions of right admiration, and as (3) the grasp of truth involves all strength of sense, evenness of judgment, and honesty of purpose, and as (4) the poetical power involves all swiftness of invention, and accuracy of historical memory, the sum of all these powers is the sum of the human soul.

Hence we see why the word " Great " is used of
this art.   It is literally great.   It compasses and
calls forth the entire human spirit, whereas any
other kind of art, being more or less small or
narrow, compasses and calls forth only *part* of
the human spirit.   Hence the idea of its magni-
tude is a literal and just one, the art being
simply less or greater in proportion to the number of faculties it exercises and addresses.*   And
this is the ultimate meaning of the definition I
gave of it long ago, as containing the "greatest
number of the greatest ideas."

Such, then, being the characters required in
order to constitute high art, if the reader will
think over them a little, and over the various
ways in which they may be falsely assumed, he
will easily perceive how spacious and dangerous
a field of discussion they open to the ambitious
critic, and of error to the ambitious artist ; he
will see how difficult it must be, either to distinguish what is truly great art from the mock-
eries of it, or to rank the real artists in anything
like a progressive system of greater and less.
For it will have been observed that the various
qualities which form greatness are partly inconsistent with each other (as some virtues are,
docility and firmness for instance), and partly

---

* Compare Stones of Venice, vol. iii. chap. iv. § 7 and
§ 21.

independent of each other ; and the fact is, that artists differ not more by mere capacity, than by the component *elements* of their capacity, each possessing in very different proportions the several attributes of greatness ; so that, classed by one kind of merit, as, for instance, purity of expression, Angelico will stand highest ; classed by another, sincerity of manner, Veronese will stand highest; classed by another, love of beauty, Leonardo will stand highest; and so on; hence arise continual disputes and misunderstandings among those who think that high art must always be one and the same, and that great artists ought to unite all great attributes in an equal degree.

In one of the exquisitely finished tales of Marmontel, a company of critics are received at dinner by the hero of the story, an old gentleman, somewhat vain of his *acquired* taste, and his niece, by whose incorrigible *natural* taste, he is seriously disturbed and tormented. During the entertainment, "On parcourut tous les genres de littérature, et pour donner plus d'essor à l'érudition et à la critique, on mit sur le tapis cette question toute neuve, sçavoir, lequel méritoit le préférence de Corneille ou de Racine. L'on disoit même là-dessus les plus belles choses du monde, lorsque la petite nièce, qui n'avoit pas dit un mot, s'avisa de demander naïvement lequel

des deux fruits, de l'orange ou de la pêche, avoit
le goût les plus exquis et méritoit le plus d'éloges.
Son oncle rougit de sa simplicité, et les convives
baissèrent tous les yeux sans daigner répondre à
cette bêtise. Ma nièce, dit Fintac, à votre
âge, il faut sçavoir écouter, et se taire."

I cannot close this chapter with shorter or
better advice to the reader, than merely, whenever he hears discussions about the relative
merits of great masters, to remember the young
lady's question. It is, indeed, true that there *is*
a relative merit, that a peach is nobler than a
hawthorn berry, and still more a hawthorn berry
than a bead of the nightshade; but in each rank
of fruits, as in each rank of masters, one is endowed with one virtue, and another with another; their glory is their dissimilarity, and they
who propose to themselves in the training of an
artist that he should unite the coloring of Tintoret, the finish of Albert Durer, and the tenderness of Correggio, are no wiser than a horti-
culturist would be, who made it the object of
his labor to produce a fruit which should unite
in itself the lusciousness of the grape, the crisp-
ness of the nut, and the fragrance of the pine.

And from these considerations one most important practical corollary is to be deduced,
with the good help of Mademoiselle Agathe's
simile, namely, that the greatness or smallness

of a man is, in the most conclusive sense, determined for him at his birth, as strictly as it is determined for a fruit whether it is to be a currant or an apricot. Education, favorable circumstances, resolution, and industry can do much; in a certain sense they do *everything;* that is to say, they determine whether the poor apricot shall fall in the form of a green bead, blighted by an east wind, shall be trodden under foot, or whether it shall expand into tender pride, and sweet brightness of golden velvet. But apricot out of currant,—great man out of small,—did never yet art or effort make; and, in a general way, men have their excellence nearly fixed for them when they are born; a little cramped and frost-bitten on one side, a little sun-burnt and fortune-spotted on the other, they reach, between good and evil chances, such size and taste as generally belong to the men of their calibre, and the small in their serviceable bunches, the great in their golden isolation, have, these no cause for regret, nor those for disdain.

Therefore it is, that every system of teaching is false which holds forth "great art" as in any wise to be taught to students, or even to be aimed at by them. Great art is precisely that which never was, nor will be taught, it is preeminently and finally the expression of the spirits of great men; so that the only wholesome teaching is that which simply endeavors to fix those characters of nobleness in the pupil's mind of which it seems easily susceptible; and without holding out to him, as a possible or even probable result, that he should ever paint like Titian, or carve like Michael Angelo, enforces upon him the manifest possibility, and assured duty, of endeavoring to draw in a manner at least honest and intelligible; and cultivates in him those general charities of heart, sincerities of thought, and graces of habit which are likely to lead him, throughout life, to prefer openness to affectation, realities to shadows, and beauty to corruption.

THE FALSE IDEAL.

The pursuit, by the imagination, of beautiful and strange thoughts or subjects, to the exclusion of painful or common ones, is called among us, in these modern days, the pursuit of "*the ideal;*" nor does any subject deserve more attentive examination than the manner in which this pursuit is entered upon by the modern mind. The reader must pardon me for making in the outset one or two statements which may appear to him somewhat wide of the matter, but which (if he admits their truth), he will, I think, presently perceive to reach to the root of it. Namely,

That men's proper business in this world falls mainly into three divisions:

First, to know themselves, and the existing state of the things they have to do with.

Secondly, to be happy in themselves, and in the existing state of things.

Thirdly, to mend themselves, and the existing state of things, as far as either are marred or mendable.

These, I say, are the three plain divisions of proper human business on this earth. For these three, the following are usually substituted and adopted by human creatures:

First, to be totally ignorant of themselves, and the existing state of things.

Secondly, to be miserable in themselves, and in the existing state of things.

Thirdly, to let themselves, and the existing state of things, alone (at least in the way of correction).

The dispositions which induce us to manage, thus wisely, the affairs of this life seem to be:

First, a fear of disagreeable facts, and conscious shrinking from clearness of light, which keep us from examining ourselves, and increase gradually into a species of instinctive terror at all truth, and love of glosses, veils, and decorative lies of every sort.

Secondly, a general readiness to take delight

in anything past, future, far off, or somewhere else, rather than in things now, near, and here leading us gradually to place our pleasure principally in the exercise of the imagination, and to build all our satisfaction on things as they are *not*. Which power being one not accorded to the lower animals, and having indeed, when disciplined, a very noble use, we pride ourselves upon it, whether disciplined or not, and pass our lives complacently, in substantial discontent, and visionary satisfaction.

Now *nearly* all artistical and poetical seeking after the ideal is only one branch of this base habit—the abuse of the imagination, in allowing it to find its whole delight in the impossible and untrue; while the faithful pursuit of the ideal is an honest use of the imagination, giving full power and presence to the possible and true.

It is the difference between these two uses of it which we have to examine.

And, first, consider what are the legitimate uses of the imagination, that is to say, of the power of perceiving, or conceiving with the mind things which cannot be perceived by the senses.

Its first and noblest use is, to enable us to bring sensibly to our sight the things which are recorded as belonging to our future state, or as invisibly surrounding us in this. It is given us, that we may imagine the cloud of witnesses in heaven and earth, and see, as if they were now present, the souls of the righteous waiting for us; that we may conceive the great army of the inhabitants of heaven, and discover among them those whom we most desire to be with for ever; that we may be able to vision forth the ministry of angels beside us, and see the chariots of fire on the mountains that gird us round; but above all, to call up the scenes and facts in which we are commanded to believe, and be present, as if in the body, at every recorded event of the history of the Redeemer. Its second and ordinary use is to empower us to traverse the scenes of all other history, and force the facts to become again visible, so as to make upon us the same impression which they would have made if we had witnessed them; and in the minor necessities of life, to enable us, out of any present good, to gather the utmost measure of enjoyment by investing it with happy associations, and, in any present evil, to lighten it, by summoning back the images of other hours; and, also, to give to all mental truths some visible type in allegory, simile, or personification, which shall more deeply enforce them; and, finally, when the mind is utterly out-wearied, to refresh it with such innocent play as shall be most in harmony with the suggestive voices of natural things, permitting it to possess living companionship instead of silent beauty, and create for itself fairies in the grass and naiads in the wave.

These being the uses of imagination, its abuses are either in creating, for mere pleasure, false images, where it is its *duty* to create true ones; or in turning what was intended for the mere refreshment of the heart into its daily food, and changing the innocent pastimes of an hour into the guilty occupation of a life.

It became necessary, to the full display of all the power of the artist, that the subject should in many respects be more faithfully imagined that it had been hitherto. "Keeping," "Expression," "Historical Unity," and such other requirements, were enforced on the painter, in the same tone, and with the same purpose, as the purity of his oil and the accuracy of his perspective. He was told that the figure of Christ should be "dignified," those of the Apostles "expressive," that of the Virgin "modest," and those of children "innocent." All this was perfectly true ; and in obedience to such directions, the painter proceeded to manufacture certain arrangements of apostolic sublimity, virginal mildness, and infantine innocence, which, being free from the quaint imperfection and contradictoriness of the early art, were looked upon by the European public as true things, and trustworthy representations of the events of religious history. The pictures of Francia and Bellini had been received as pleasant visions. But the cartoons of Raphael were received as representations of historical fact.

Now, neither they, nor any other work of the period, were representations either of historical or possible fact. They were, in the strictest sense of the word, "compositions"—cold arrangements of propriety and agreeableness, according to academical formulas; the painter never in any case making the slightest effort to conceive the thing as it must have happened, but only to gather together graceful lines and beautiful faces, in such compliance with commonplace ideas of the subject as might obtain for the whole an "epic unity," or some such other form of scholastic perfectness.

Take a very important instance.

I suppose there is no event in the whole life of Christ to which, in hours of doubt or fear, men turn with more anxious thirst to know the close facts of it, or with more earnest and passionate dwelling upon every syllable of its recorded narrative, than Christ's showing Himself to his disciples at the lake of Galilee. There is something pre-eminently open, natural, full fronting our disbelief in this manifestation. The others, recorded after the resurrection, were sudden, phantom-like, occurring to men in profound sorrow and wearied agitation of heart; not, it might seem, safe judges of what they saw. But the agitation was now over. They had gone back to their daily work, thinking still their business lay net-wards, unmeshed from the literal rope and drag. "Simon Peter saith unto them, 'I go a-fishing.' They say unto him, 'We also go with thee.'" True words enough, and having far echo beyond those Galilean hills. That night they caught nothing; but when the morning came, in the clear light of it, behold a figure stood on the shore. They were not thinking of anything but their fruitless hauls. They had no guess who it was. It asked them simply if they had caught anything. They said no. And it tells them to cast yet again. And John shades his eyes from the morning sun with his hand, to look who it is; and though the glinting of the sea, too, dazzles him, he makes out who it is, at last; and poor Simon, not to be outrun this time, tightens his fisher's coat about him, and dashes in, over the nets. One would have liked to see him swim those hundred yards, and stagger to his knees on the beach.

Well, the others get to the beach, too, in time, in such slow way as men in general do get, in this world, to its true shore, much impeded by that wonderful "dragging the net with fishes;"

but they get there—seven of them in all ;—first the Denier, and then the slowest believer, and then the quickest believer, and then the two throne-seekers, and two more, we know not who.

They sit down on the shore face to face with Him, and eat their broiled fish as He bids. And then, to Peter, all dripping still, shivering, and amazed, staring at Christ in the sun on the other side of the coal fire,—thinking a little, perhaps, of what happened by another coal fire, when it was colder, and having had no word once changed with him by his Master since that look of His,—to him, so amazed, comes the question, "Simon, lovest thou me?" Try to feel that a little, and think of it till it is true to you ; and then, take up that infinite monstrosity and hypocrisy—Raphael's cartoon of the Charge to Peter. Note, first, the bold fallacy—the putting *all* the Apostles there, a mere lie to serve the Papal heresy of the Petric supremacy, by putting them all in the background while Peter receives the charge, and making them all witnesses to it. Note the handsomely curled hair and neatly tied sandals of the men who had been out all night in the sea-mists and on the slimy decks. Note their convenient dresses for going a-fishing, with trains that lie a yard along the ground, and goodly fringes,—all made to match, an apostolic fishing costume.* Note how Peter especially (whose chief glory was in his wet coat *girt* about him and naked limbs) is enveloped in folds and fringes, so as to kneel and hold his keys with grace. No fire of coals at all, nor lonely mountain shore, but a pleasant Italian landscape, full of villas and churches, and a flock of sheep to be pointed at ; and the whole group of Apostles, not round Christ, as they would have been naturally, but straggling away in a line, that they may all be shown.

The simple truth is, that the moment we look at the picture we feel our belief of the whole thing taken away. There is, visibly, no possibility of that group ever having existed, in any place, or on any occasion. It is all a mere mythic absurdity, and faded concoction of fringes, muscular arms, and curly heads of Greek philosophers.

Now, the evil consequences of the acceptance of this kind of religious idealism for true, were instant and manifold. So far as it was received and trusted in by thoughtful persons, it only served to chill all the conceptions of sacred history which they might otherwise have obtained. Whatever they could have fancied for themselves

---

* I suppose Raphael intended a reference to Numbers xv. 38 ; but if he did the *blue* riband, or " vitta," as it is in the Vulgate, should have been on the borders too.

about the wild, strange, infinitely stern, infinitely tender, infinitely varied veracities of the life
of Christ, was blotted out by the vapid fineries
of Raphael ; the rough Galilean pilot, the orderly custom receiver, and all the questioning wonder and fire of uneducated apostleship, were obscured under an antique masque of philosophical
faces and long robes.   The feeble, subtle, suffering, ceaseless energy and humiliation of St. Paul
were confused with an idea of a meditative Her-
cules leaning on a sweeping sword ;* and the
mighty presences of Moses and Elias were
softened by introductions of delicate grace
adopted from dancing nymphs and rising Au-
roras.†

Now, no vigorously minded religious person
could possibly receive pleasure or help from such

---

* In the St. Cecilia of Bologna.

† In the Transfiguration. Do but try to believe that
Moses and Elias are really there talking with Christ,
Moses in the loveliest heart and midst of the land which
once it had been denied him to behold,—Elijah treading
the earth again, from which he had been swept to heaven
in fire; both now with a mightier message than ever they
had given in life,—mightier, in closing their own mission,
—mightier, in speaking to Christ " of His decease, which
He should accomplish at Jerusalem."   They, men of like
passions once with us, appointed to speak to the Redeemer of His death.

And, then, look at Raphael's kicking gracefulnesses.

art as this ; and the necessary result was the
instant rejection of it by the healthy religion of
the world. Raphael ministered, with applause,
to the impious luxury of the Vatican, but was
trampled under foot at once by every believing
and advancing Christian of his own and subsequent times ; and thenceforward pure Christianity and "high art" took separate roads, and
fared on, as best they might, independently of
each other.

But although Calvin, and Knox, and Luther,
and their flocks, with all the hardest-headed and
truest-hearted faithful left in Christendom, thus
spurned away the spurious art, and all art with
it (not without harm to themselves, such as a
man must needs sustain in cutting off a decayed
limb *), certain conditions of weaker Christianity
suffered the false system to retain influence over
them; and to this day, the clear and tasteless
poison of the art of Raphael infects with sleep
of infidelity the hearts of millions of Christians.
It is the first cause of all that pre-eminent *dulness* which characterizes what Protestants call
sacred art; a dulness, not merely baneful in
making religion distasteful to the young, but in
sickening, as we have seen, all vital belief of re-

---

* Luther had no dislike of religious art on principle.
Even the stove in his chamber was wrought with sacred
subjects. See Mrs. Stowe's Sunny Memories.

ligion in the old. A dim sense of impossibility
attaches itself always to the graceful emptiness
of the representation; we feel instinctively that
the painted Christ and painted apostle are not
beings that ever did or could exist; and this
fatal sense of fair fabulousness, and well-com-
posed impossibility, steals gradually from the
picture into the history, until we find ourselves
reading St. Mark or St. Luke with the same admiring, but uninterested, incredulity, with which
we contemplate Raphael.

On a certain class of minds, however, these
Raphaelesque and other sacred paintings of high
order, have had, of late years, another kind of
influence, much resembling that which they
had at first on the most pious Romanists.
They are used to excite certain conditions of
religious dream or reverie; being again, as in
earliest times, regarded not as representations of
fact, but as expressions of sentiment respecting
the fact. In this way the best of them have
unquestionably much purifying and enchanting
power; and they are helpful opponents to sinful
passion and weakness of every kind. A fit of
unjust anger, petty malice, unreasonable vexa-
tion, or dark passion, cannot certainly, in a mind
of ordinary sensibility, hold its own in the presence of a good engraving from any work of
Angelico, Memling, or Perugino. But I never-

theless believe, that he who trusts much to such
helps will find them fail him at his need ; and
that the dependence, in any great degree, on
the presence or power of a picture, indicates a
wonderfully feeble sense of the presence and
power of God. I do not think that any man,
who is thoroughly certain that Christ is in the
room, will care what sort of pictures of Christ
he has on its walls; and, in the plurality of
cases, the delight taken in art of this kind is, in
reality, nothing more than a form of graceful indulgence of those sensibilities which the habits
of a disciplined life restrain in other directions.
Such art is, in a word, the opera and drama of
the monk. Sometimes it is worse than this,
and the love of it is the mask under which a
general thirst for morbid excitement will pass
itself for religion. The young lady who rises in
the middle of the day, jaded by her last night's
ball, and utterly incapable of any simple or
wholesome religious exercise, can still gaze into
the dark eyes of the Madonna di San Sisto, or
dream over the whiteness of an ivory crucifix,
and return to the course of her daily life in full
persuasion that her morning's feverishness has
atoned for her evening's folly. And all the
while, the art which possesses these very doubtful advantages is acting for undoubtful detri-
ment, in the various ways above examined, on

the inmost fastnesses of faith; it is throwing subtle endearments round foolish traditions, confusing sweet fancies with sound doctrines, obscuring real events with unlikely semblances, and enforcing false assertions with pleasant circumstantiality, until, to the usual, and assuredly sufficient, difficulties standing in the way of belief, its votaries have added a habit of sentimentally changing what they know to be true, and of dearly loving what they confess to be false.

Has there, then (the reader asks emphatically), been *no* true religious ideal? Has religious art never been of any service to mankind? I fear, on the whole, not. Of true religious ideal, representing events historically recorded, with solemn effect at a sincere and unartificial conception, there exist, as yet, hardly any examples. Nearly all good religious pictures fall into one or other branch of the false ideal already examined, either into the Angelican (passionate ideal) or the Raphaelesque (philosophical ideal). But there is one true form of religious art, nevertheless, in the pictures of the passionate ideal which represent imaginary beings of another world. Since it is evidently right that we should try to imagine the glories of the next world, and as this imagination must be, in each separate mind, more or less different,

and unconfined by any laws of material fact, the
passionate ideal has not only full scope here,
but it becomes our duty to urge its powers to
its utmost, so that every condition of beautiful
form and color may be employed to invest these
scenes with greater delightfulness (the whole
being, of course, received as an assertion of possibility, not of absolute fact).   All the paradises
imagined by the religious painters—the choirs
of glorified saints, angels, and spiritual powers,
when painted with full belief in this possibility
of their existence, are true ideals, and so far
from our having dwelt on these too much, I believe, rather, we have not trusted them enough,
nor accepted them enough, as possible statements of most precious truth.   Nothing but
unmixed good can accrue to any mind from the
contemplation of Orcagna's Last Judgment or
his triumph of death, of Angelico's Last Judgment and Paradise, or any of the scenes laid in
heaven by the other faithful religious masters;
and the more they are considered, not as works
of art, but as real visions of real things, more or
less imperfectly set down, the more good will be
got by dwelling upon them.   The same is true
of representations of Christ as a living presence
among us now, as in Hunt's Light of the World.

The examination of the various degrees in
which sacred art has reached its proper power is

not to our present purpose; still less, to investigate the infinitely difficult question of its past operation on the Christian mind; it being enough here to mark the forms of ideal error, without historically tracing their extent, and to state generally that my impression is, up to the present moment, that the best religious art has been *hitherto* rather a fruit, and attending sign, of sincere Christianity than a promoter of or help to it. More, I think, has always been done for God by few words than many pictures, and more by few acts than many words.

I must not, however, quit the subject without insisting on the chief practical consequence of what we have observed, namely, that sacred art, so far from being exhausted, has yet to attain the development of its highest branches; and the task, or privilege, yet remains for mankind, to produce an art which shall be at once entirely skilful and entirely *sincere*. All the histories of the Bible are, in my judgment, yet waiting to be painted. Moses has never been painted; Elijah never; David never (except as a mere ruddy stripling); Deborah never; Gideon never; Isaiah never. What single example does the reader remember of painting which suggested so much as the faintest shadow of these people, or of their deeds? Strong men in armor, or aged men with flowing beards, he *may* remember,

who, when he looked at his Louvre or Uffizii
catalogue, he found were intended to stand for
David or for Moses.   But does he suppose that,
if these pictures had suggested to him the fee-
blest image of the presence of such men, he
would have passed on, as he assuredly did, to the
next picture,—representing, doubtless, Diana and
Actæon, or Cupid and the graces, or a gambling
quarrel in a pothouse,—with no sense of pain,
or surprise?   Let him meditate over the matter,
and he will find ultimately that what I say is
true, and that religious art, at once complete
and sincere, never yet has existed.

It will exist: nay, I believe the era of its birth
has come, and that those bright Turnerian im-
ageries, which the European public declared to
be "dotage," and those calm Pre-Raphaelite
studies which, in like manner, it pronounced
"puerility," form the first foundation that has
been ever laid for true sacred art.   Of this we
shall presently reason farther.   But, be it as it
may, if we would cherish the hope that sacred
art may, indeed, arise for *us*, two separate cau-
tions are to be addressed to the two opposed
classes of religionists whose influence will chiefly
retard that hope's accomplishment.   The group
calling themselves Evangelical ought no longer
to render their religion an offence to men of the
world by associating it only with the most vul-

gar forms of art. It is not necessary that they should admit either music or painting into religious service; but, if they admit either the one or the other, let it not be bad music nor bad painting : it is certainly in nowise more for Christ's honor that His praise should be sung discordantly, or His miracles painted discreditably, than that His word should be preached ungrammatically. Some Evangelicals, however, seem to take a morbid pride in the triple degradation.*

The opposite class of men, whose natural instincts lead them to mingle the refinements of art with all the offices and practices of religion, are to be warned, on the contrary, how they

---

* I do not know anything more humiliating to a man of common sense, than to open what is called an " Illustrated Bible " of modern days. See, for instance, the plates in Brown's Bible (octavo : Edinburgh, 1840), a standard evangelical edition. Our habit of reducing the Psalms to doggerel before we will condescend to sing them, is a parallel abuse. It is marvellous to think that human creatures with tongues and souls should refuse to chant the verse: " Before Ephraim, Benjamin, and Manasseh, stir up thy strength, and come and help us;" preferring this:—

" Behold, how Benjamin expects,
   With Ephraim and Manasseh joined,
  In their deliverance, the effects
   Of thy resistless strength to find!"

mistake their enjoyments for their duties, or confound poetry with faith. I admit that it is impossible for one man to judge another in this matter, and that it can never be said with certainty how far what seems frivolity may be force, and what seems the indulgence of the heart may be, indeed, its dedication. I am ready to believe that Metastasio, expiring in a canzonet, may have died better than if his prayer had been in unmeasured syllables.* But, for the most part, it is assuredly much to be feared lest we mistake a surrender to the charms of art for one to the service of God; and, in the art which we permit, lest we substitute sentiment for sense, grace for utility. And for us all there is in this matter even a deeper danger than that of indulgence. There is the danger of Artistical Pharisaism. Of all the forms of pride and vanity, as there are none more subtle, so I believe

---

* " En 1780, âgé de quartre-vingt-deux ans, au moment de recevoir le viatique, il rassembla ses forces, et chanta à son Créateur

> ' Eterno Genitor
> Io t' offro il proprio figlio
> Che in pegno del tuo amor
> Si vuole a me donar.
> A lui rivolgi il ciglio,
> Mira chi t' offro; e poi,
> Niega, Signor, se puoi,
> Niegr di perdonar.' "

—DE STENDHAL. *Via de Metastasio.*

there are none more sinful, than those which are manifested by the Pharisees of art. To be proud of birth, of place, of wit, of bodily beauty, is comparatively innocent, just because such pride is more natural, and more easily detected. But to be proud of our sanctities; to pour contempt upon our fellows, because, forsooth, we like to look at Madonnas in bowers of roses, better than at plain pictures of plain things: and to make this religious art of ours the expression of our own perpetual self-complacency,—congratulating ourselves, day by day, on our purities, proprieties, elevations, and inspirations, as above the reach of common mortals,—this I believe to be one of the wickedest and foolishest forms of human egotism; and, truly, I had rather, with great, thoughtless, humble Paul Veronese, make the Supper at Emmaus a background for two children playing with a dog (as, God knows, men do usually put it in the background to everything, if not out of sight altogether), than join that school of modern Germanism which wears its pieties for decoration as women wear their diamonds, and flaunts the dry fleeces of its phylacteries between its dust and the dew of heaven.

When we pass to the examination of what is beautiful and expressive in art, we shall fre-

quently find distinctive qualities in the minds
even of inferior artists, which have led them to
the pursuit and embodying of particular trains
of thought, altogether different from those which
direct the compositions of other men, and incapable of comparison with them. Now, when
this is the case, we should consider it in the
highest degree both invidious and illogical, to
say of such different modes of exertion of the
intellect, that one is in all points greater or
nobler than another. We shall probably find
something in the working of all minds which has
an end and a power peculiar to itself, and which
is deserving of free and full admiration without
any reference whatsoever to what has, in other
fields, been accomplished by other modes of
thought, and directions of aim. We shall,
indeed, find a wider range and grasp in one
man than in another; but yet it will be our own
fault if we do not discover something in the
most limited range of mind which is different
from, and in its way better than, anything presented to us by the more grasping intellect.
We all know that the nightingale sings more
nobly than the lark; but who, therefore, would
wish the lark not to sing, or would deny that it
had a character of its own, which bore a part
among the melodies of creation no less essential
than that of the more richly-gifted bird? And

thus we shall find and feel that whatever difference may exist between the intellectual powers of one artist and another, yet wherever there is any true genius, there will be some peculiar lesson which even the humblest will teach us more sweetly and perfectly than those far above them in prouder attributes of mind; and we should be as mistaken as we should be unjust and invidious, if we refused to receive this their peculiar message with gratitude and veneration, merely because it was a sentence and not a volume. But the case is different when we examine their relative fidelity to given facts. That fidelity depends on no peculiar modes of thought or habits of character; it is the result of keen sensibility, combined with high powers of memory and association. These qualities, as such, are the same in all men; character or feeling may direct their choice to this or that object, but the fidelity with which they treat either the one or the other, is dependent on those simple powers of sense and intellect which are like and comparable in all, and of which we can always say that they are greater in this man, or less in that, without reference to the character of the individual.

I believe there is nearly as much occasion, at the present day, for advocacy of Michael Angelo against the pettiness of the moderns, as there is

for support of Turner against the conventionalities of the ancients.   For, though the names of
the fathers of sacred art are on all our lips, our
faith in them is much like that of the great world
in its religion—nominal, but dead.   In vain our
lecturers sound the name of Raffaelle in the ears
of their pupils, while their own works are visibly
at variance with every principle deducible from
his.   In vain is the young student compelled to
produce a certain number of school copies of
Michael Angelo, when his bread must depend
on the number of gewgaws he can crowd into
his canvas.   And I could with as much zeal ex-
ert myself against the modern system of English
historical art, as I have in favor of our school of
landscape, but that it is an ungrateful and painful task to attack the works of living painters,
struggling with adverse circumstances of every
kind, and especially with the false taste of a nation which regards matters of art either with the
ticklishness of an infant, or the stolidity of a
Megatherium.

Now, there is but one grand style, in the treatment of all subjects whatsoever, and that style
is based on the *perfect* knowledge, and consists
ın the simple, unencumbered rendering, of the
specific characters of the given object, be it man,
beast, or flower.   Every change, caricature, or

abandonment of such specific character, is as destructive of grandeur as it is of truth, of beauty as of propriety. Every alteration of the features of nature has its origin either in powerless indolence or blind audacity, in the folly which forgets, or the insolence which desecrates, works which it is the pride of angels to know and their privilege to love.

Painting, or art generally, as such, with all its technicalities, difficulties, and particular ends, is nothing but a noble and expressive language, invaluable as the vehicle of thought, but by itself nothing. He who has learned what is commonly considered the whole art of painting, that is, the art of representing any natural object faithfully, has as yet only learned the language by which his thoughts are to be expressed. He has done just as much towards being that which we ought to respect as a great painter, as a man who has learned how to express himself grammatically and melodiously has towards being a great poet. The language is, indeed, more difficult of acquirement in the one case than in the other, and possesses more power of delighting the sense, while it speaks to the intellect, but it is, nevertheless, nothing more than language, and all those excellences which are peculiar to the painter as such, are merely what rhythm, melody, precision and force are in the words of the orator and the poet, necessary to their greatness, but not the tests of their greatness. It is not by the mode of representing and saying, but by what is represented and said, that the respective greatness either of the painter or the writer is to be finally determined.

Speaking with strict propriety, therefore, we should call a man a great painter only as he excelled in precision and force in the language of lines, and a great versifier, as he excelled in precision or force in the language of words. A great poet would then be a term strictly, and in precisely the same sense applicable to both, if warranted by the character of the images or thoughts which each in their respective languages conveyed.

Take, for instance, one of the most perfect poems or pictures (I use the words as synonymous) which modern times have seen:—the "Old Shepherd's Chief-mourner." Here the exquisite execution of the glossy and crisp hair of the dog, the bright sharp touching of the green bough beside it, the clear painting of the wood of the coffin and the folds of the blanket, are language—language clear and expressive in the highest degree. But the close pressure of the dog's breast against the wood, the convulsive clinging of the paws, which has dragged the blanket off the trestle, the total powerlessness of the head laid, close and motionless, upon its folds, the fixed and tearful fall of the eye in its utter hopelessness, the rigidity of repose which marks that there has been no motion nor change in the trance of agony since the last blow was struck on the coffin-lid, the quietness and gloom of the chamber, the spectacles marking the place where the Bible was last closed, indicating how lonely has been the life—how unwatched the departure of him who is now laid solitary in his sleep;—these are all thoughts—thoughts by which the picture is separated at once from hundreds of equal merit, as far as mere painting goes, by which it ranks as a work of high art, and stamps its author, not as the neat imitator of the texture of a skin, or the fold of a drapery, but as the Man of Mind.

It must be the part of the judicious critic carefully to distinguish what is language, and what is thought, and to rank and praise pictures chiefly for the latter, considering the former as a totally inferior excellence, and one which cannot be compared with nor weighed against thought in any way nor in any degree whatsoever. The picture which has the nobler anc more numerous ideas, however awkwardly expressed, is a greater and a better picture thar that which has the less noble and less numerou ideas, however beautifully expressed. No weight, nor mass, nor beauty of execution can outweigh one grain or fragment of thought. Three pen-strokes of Raffaelle are a greater and a better picture than the most finished work that ever Carlo Dolci polished into inanity. A finished work of a great artist is only better than its sketch, if the sources of pleasure belonging to color and realization—valuable in themselves,—are so employed as to increase the impressiveness of the thought. But if one atom of thought has vanished, all color, all finish, all execution, all ornament, are too dearly bought. Nothing but thought can pay for thought, and the instant that the increasing refinement or finish of the picture begins to be paid for by the loss of the faintest shadow of an idea, that instant all refinement or finish is an excrescence, and a deformity.

I think that all the sources of pleasure, or any other good, to be derived from works of art, may be referred to five distinct heads.

 I. Ideas of Power.—The perception or conception of the mental or bodily powers by which the work has been produced.

 II. Ideas of Imitation.—The perception that the thing produced resembles something else.

 III. Ideas of Truth.—The perception of faith-

fulness in a statement of facts by the
thing produced.

IV. Ideas of Beauty.—The perception of
beauty, either in the thing produced, or
in what it suggests or resembles.

V. Ideas of Relation.—The perception of intellectual relations, in the thing produced,
or in what it suggests or resembles.

I shall briefly distinguish the nature and effects of each of these classes of ideas.

———◆———

I.—IDEAS OF POWER.

These are the simple perception of the
mental or bodily powers exerted in the production of any work of art. According to
the dignity and degree of the power perceived is the dignity of the idea; but the whole
class of ideas is received by the intellect, and
they excite the best of the moral feelings, veneration, and the desire of exertion. Men may
let their great powers lie dormant, while they
employ their mean and petty powers on mean
and petty objects, but it is physically impossible
to employ a great power, except on a great object. Consequently, wherever power of any kind
or degree has been exerted, the marks and evi-

dence of it are stamped upon its results: it is impossible that it should be lost or wasted, or without record, even in the "estimation of a hair:" and therefore, whatever has been the subject of a great power, bears about with it the image of that which created it, and is what is commonly called "excellent." And this is the true meaning of the word excellent, as distinguished from the terms, "beautiful," "useful," "good," etc.; and we shall always, in future, use the word excellent, as signifying that the thing to which it is applied required a great power for its production.

———◆———

II. IDEAS OF IMITATION.

Whenever anything looks like what it is not, the resemblance being so great as *nearly* to deceive, we feel a kind of pleasurable surprise, an agreeable excitement of mind, exactly the same in its nature as that which we receive from juggling. Whenever we perceive this in something produced by art, that is to say, whenever the work is seen to resemble something which we know it is not, we receive what I call an idea of imitation. *Why* such ideas are pleasing, it would be out of our present purpose to inquire; we only know that there is no man who does not feel pleasure in his animal nature from gentle surprise, and that such surprise can be excited in no more distinct manner than by the evidence that a thing is not what it appears to be. Now two things are requisite to our complete and more pleasurable perception of this: first, that the resemblance be so perfect as to amount to a deception; secondly, that there be some means of proving at the same moment that it *is* a deception. The most perfect ideas and pleasures of imitation are, therefore, when one sense is contradicted by another, both bearing as positive evidence on the subject as each is capable of alone; as when the eye says a thing is round, and the finger says it is flat; they are, therefore, never felt in so high a degree as in painting, where appearance of projection, roughness, hair, velvet, etc., are given with a smooth surface, or in waxwork, where the first evidence of the senses is perpetually contradicted by their experience; but the moment we come to marble, our definition checks us, for a marble figure does not look like what it is not; it looks like marble, and like the form of a man, but then it *is* marble, and it *is* the form of a man. It does not look like a man, which it is not, but like the form of a man, which it is. Form is form, *bond fide* and actual, whether in marble or in flesh—

not an imitation or resemblance of form, but real form. The chalk outline of the bough of a tree on paper, is not an imitation; it looks like chalk and paper—not like wood, and that which it suggests to the mind is not properly said to be *like* the form of a bough, it *is* the form of a bough.

III.—IDEAS OF TRUTH.

The word truth, as applied to art, signifies the faithful statement, either to the mind or senses, of any fact of nature.

We receive an idea of truth, then, when we perceive the faithfulness of such a statement.

The difference between ideas of truth and of imitation lies chiefly in the following points.

First,—Imitation can only be of something material, but truth has reference to statements both of the qualities of material things, and of emotions, impressions, and thoughts. There is a moral as well as material truth,—a truth of impression as well as of form,—of thought as well as of matter; and the truth of impression and thought is a thousand times the more important of the two. Hence, truth is a term of universal application, but imitation is limited to that narrow field of art which takes cognizance only of material things.

Secondly,—Truth may be stated by any signs or symbols which have a definite signification in the minds of those to whom they are addressed, although such signs be themselves no image nor likeness of anything. Whatever can excite in the mind the conception of certain facts, can give ideas of truth, though it be in no degree the imitation or resemblance of those facts. If there be—we do not say there is,—but if there be in painting anything which operates, as words do, not by resembling anything, but by being taken as a symbol and substitute for it, and thus inducing the effect of it, then this channel of communication can convey uncorrupted truth, though it do not in any degree resemble the facts whose conception it induces. But ideas of imitation, of course, require the likeness of the object. They speak to the perceptive faculties only: truth to the conceptive.

Thirdly,—And in consequence of what is above stated, an idea of truth exists in the statement of *one* attribute of anything, but an idea of imitation requires the resemblance of as many attributes as we are usually cognizant of in its real presence.

The other day at Bruges, while I was endeavoring to set down in my notebook something of

the ineffable expression of the Madonna in the
cathedral, a French amateur came up to me, to
inquire if I had seen the modern French pictures
in a neighboring church. I had not, but felt
little inclined to leave my marble for all the canvas that ever suffered from French brushes. My
apathy was attacked with gradually increasing
energy of praise. Rubens never executed—
Titian never colored anything like them. I
thought this highly probable, and still sat quiet.
The voice continued at my ear. " Parbleu, Monsieur, Michel Ange n'a rien produit de plus
beau !" "De plus *beau ?*" repeated I, wishing
to know what particular excellences of Michael
Angelo were to be intimated by this expression.
"Monsieur, on ne peut plus—c'est un tableau
admirable—inconcevable: Monsieur," said the
Frenchman, lifting up his hands to heaven, as he
concentrated in one conclusive and overwhelm-
ing proposition the qualities which were to out-
shine Rubens and overpower Buonaroti,—"Monsieur, IL SORT !"

This gentleman could only perceive two truths
—flesh color and projection. These constituted
his notion of the perfection of painting; because
they unite all that is necessary for deception.
He was not therefore cognizant of many ideas of
truth, though perfectly cognizant of ideas of imitation.

IV.—IDEAS OF BEAUTY.

Ideas of beauty are among the noblest which can be presented to the human mind, invariably exalting and purifying it according to their degree; and it would appear that we are intended by the Deity to be constantly under their influence, because there is not one single object in nature which is not capable of conveying them, and which to the rightly perceiving mind does not present an incalculably greater number of beautiful than of deformed parts; there being in fact scarcely anything in pure, undiseased nature, like positive deformity, but only degrees of beauty, or such slight and rare points of permitted contrast as may render all around them more valuable by their opposition; spots of blackness in creation, to make its colors felt.

———◆———

V.—IDEAS OF RELATION.

Under this head must be arranged everything productive of expression, sentiment, and character, whether in figures or landscapes (for there may be as much definite expression and marked carrying out of particular thoughts in the treat-

ment of inanimate as of animate nature), everything relating to the conception of the subject
and to the congruity and relation of its parts;
not as they enhance each other's beauty by
known and constant laws of composition, but as
they give each other expression and meaning,
by particular application, requiring distinct
thought to discover or to enjoy: the choice, for
instance, of a particular lurid or appalling light,
to illustrate an incident in itself terrible, or of a
particular tone of pure color to prepare the mind
for the expression of refined and delicate feeling; and, in a still higher sense, the invention of
such incidents and thoughts as can be expressed
in words as well as on canvas, and are totally independent of any means of art but such as may
serve for the bare suggestion of them. The
principal object in the foreground of Turner's
" Building of Carthage " is a group of children
sailing toy boats. The exquisite choice of this
incident, as expressive of the ruling passion,
which was to be the source of future greatness,
in preference to the tumult of busy stone-ma-
sons or arming soldiers, is quite as appreciable
when it is told as when it is seen,—it has nothing to do with the technicalities of painting; a
scratch of the pen would have conveyed the idea
and spoken to the intellect as much as the elaborate realizations of color. Such a thought as

this is something far above all art; it is epic poetry of the highest order.

By the term "ideas of relation," then, I mean in future to express all those sources of pleasure, which involve and require, at the instant of their perception, active exertion of the intellectual powers.

Sublimity is not a specific term,—not a term descriptive of the effect of a particular class of ideas. Anything which elevates the mind is sublime, and the elevation of mind is produced by the contemplation of greatness of any kind; but chiefly, of course, by the greatness of the noblest things. Sublimity is, therefore, only another word for the effect of greatness upon the feelings. Greatness of matter, space, power, virtue, or beauty, are thus all sublime; and there is perhaps no desirable quality of a work of art, which in its perfection is not, in some way or degree, sublime.

I am fully prepared to allow of much ingenu ity in Burke's theory of the sublime, as connected with self-preservation. There are few things so great as death; and there is perhaps nothing which banishes all littleness of thought and feeling in an equal degree with its contemplation. Everything, therefore, which in any way points to it, and, therefore, most dangers and powers over which we have little control, are in some

degree sublime.   But it is not the fear, observe,
but the contemplation of death; not the instinctive shudder and struggle of self-preservation,
but the deliberate measurement of the doom,
which are really great or sublime in feeling.   It
is not while we shrink, but while we defy, that
we receive or convey the highest conceptions of
the fate.   There is no sublimity in the agony of
terror.   Whether do we trace it most in the cry
to the mountains, " fall on us," and to the hills,
" cover us," or in the calmness of the prophecy
—" And though after my skin worms destroy
this body, yet in my flesh I shall see God "?   A
little reflection will easily convince any one, that
so far from the feelings of self-preservation being necessary to the sublime, their greatest action is totally destructive of it; and that there
are few feelings less capable of its perception
than those of a coward.   But the simple conception or idea of greatness of suffering or extent
of destruction is sublime, whether there be any
connection of that idea with ourselves or not.
If we were placed beyond the reach of all peril
or pain, the perception of these agencies in their
influence on others would not be less sublime,
not because peril or pain are sublime in their
own nature, but because their contemplation, exciting compassion or fortitude, elevates the mind,
and renders meanness of thought impossible.

The truths of nature are one eternal change—one infinite variety. There is no bush on the face of the globe exactly like another bush;—there are no two trees in the forest whose boughs bend into the same network, nor two leaves on the same tree which could not be told one from the other, nor two waves in the sea exactly alike. And out of this mass of various, yet agreeing beauty, it is by long attention only that the conception of the constant character—the ideal form—hinted at by all, yet assumed by none, is fixed upon the imagination for its standard of truth.

It is not singular, therefore, nor in any way disgraceful, that the majority of spectators are totally incapable of appreciating the truth of nature, when fully set before them; but it is both singular and disgraceful that it is so difficult to convince them of their own incapability. Ask the connoisseur, who has scampered over all Europe, the shape of the leaf of an elm, and the chances are ninety to one that he cannot tell you; and yet he will be voluble of criticism on every painted landscape from Dresden to Madrid, and pretend to tell you whether they are like nature or not. Ask an enthusiastic chatterer in the Sistine Chapel, how many ribs he has, and you get no answer; but it is odds that you do not get out of the door without his

informing you that he considers such and such
a figure badly drawn!

A few such interrogations as these might indeed convict, if not convince the mass of spectators of incapability, were it not for the universal reply, that they can recognize what they cannot describe, and feel what is truthful, though
they do not know what is truth. And this is,
to a certain degree, true; a man may recognize
the portrait of his friend, though he cannot, if
you ask him apart, tell you the shape of his nose
or the height of his forehead; and every one
could tell Nature herself from an imitation;
why not then, it will be asked, what is like her
from what is not? For this simple reason, that
we constantly recognize things by their least important attributes, and by the help of very few
of those: and if these attributes exist not in the
imitation, though there may be thousands of
others far higher and more valuable, yet if those
be wanting, or imperfectly rendered, by which
we are accustomed to recognize the object, we
deny the likeness.

Mrs. Jameson somewhere mentions the ex-
clamation of a lady of her acquaintance, more
desirous to fill a pause in conversation than
abundant in sources of observation: " What an
excellent book the Bible is!" This was a very
general truth indeed; a truth predicable of the

Bible in common with many other books, but it certainly is neither striking nor important. Had the lady exclaimed—" How evidently is the Bible a divine revelation!" she would have expressed a particular truth, one predicable of the Bible only; but certainly far more interesting and important. Had she, on the contrary, informed us that the Bible was a book, she would have been still more general, and still less entertaining. If I ask any one who somebody else is, and receive for answer that he is a man, I get little satisfaction for my pains; but if I am told that he is Sir Isaac Newton, I immediately thank my neighbor for his information. The fact is, and the above instances may serve at once to prove it if it be not self-evident, that generality gives importance to the *subject*, and limitation or particularity to the *predicate*. If I say that such and such a man in China is an opium eater, I say nothing very interesting, because my subject (such a man) is particular. If I say that all men in China are opium eaters, I say something interesting, because my subject (all men) is general. If I say that all men in China eat, I say nothing interesting, because my predicate (eat) is general. If I say that all men in China eat opium, I say something interesting, because my predicate (eat opium) is particular.

Now almost everything which (with reference

to a given subject) a painter has to ask himself whether he shall represent or not, is a predicate. Hence in art, particular truths are usually more important than general ones.

What should we think of a poet who should keep all his life repeating the same thought in different words? and why should we be more lenient to the parrot-painter who has learned one lesson from the page of nature, and keeps stammering it out with eternal repetition without turning the leaf? Is it less tautology to describe a thing over and over again with lines, than it is with words? The teaching of nature is as varied and infinite as it is constant; and the duty of the painter is to watch for every one of her lessons, and to give (for human life will admit of nothing more) those in which she has manifested each of her principles in the most peculiar and striking way. The deeper his research and the rarer the phenomena he has noted, the more valuable will his works be; to repeat himself, even in a single instance, is treachery to nature, for a thousand human lives would not be enough to give one instance of the perfect manifestation of each of her powers; and as for combining or classifying them, as well might a preacher expect in one sermon to express and explain every divine truth which can be gathered out of God's revelation, as a painter

expect in one composition to express and illustrate every lesson which can be received from
God's creation. Both are commentators on infinity, and the duty of both is to take for each
discourse one essential truth, seeking particularly and insisting especially on those which are
less palpable to ordinary observation, and more
likely to escape an indolent research ; and to
impress that, and that alone, upon those whom
they address, with every illustration that can be
furnished by their knowledge, and every adorn-
ment attainable by their power. And the real
truthfulness of the painter is in proportion to the
number and variety of the facts he has so illustrated ; those facts being always, as above observed, the realization, not the violation of a
general principle. The quantity of truth is in
proportion to the number of such facts, and its
value and instructiveness in proportion to their
rarity. All really great pictures, therefore, exhibit the general habits of nature, manifested in
some peculiar, rare, and beautiful way.

By Locke's definition of bodies, only bulk,
figure, situation, and motion or rest of solid
parts, are primary qualities. Hence all truths
of color sink at once into the second rank. He,
therefore, who has neglected a truth of form for
a truth of color, has neglected a greater truth
for a less one.

And that color is indeed a most unimportant characteristic of objects, will be farther evident on the slightest consideration. The color of plants is constantly changing with the season, and of everything with the quality of light falling on it; but the nature and essence of the thing are independent of these changes. An oak is an oak, whether green with spring or red with winter ; a dahlia is a dahlia, whether it be yellow or crimson ; and if some monster-hunting botanist should ever frighten the flower blue, still it will be a dahlia ; but let one curve of the petals—one groove of the stamens be wanting, and the flower ceases to be the same. Let the roughness of the bark and the angles of the boughs be smoothed or diminished, and the oak ceases to be an oak ; but let it retain its inward structure and outward form, and though its leaves grew white, or pink, or blue, or tri-color, it would be a white oak, or a pink oak, or a republican oak, but an oak still. Again, color is hardly ever even a *possible* distinction between two objects of the same species. Two trees, of the same kind, at the same season, and of the same age, are of absolutely the same color ; but they are not of the same form, nor anything like it. There can be no difference in the color of two pieces of rock broken from the same place ; but it is impossible they should be of the same form. So that form is not only the chief characteristic of species, but the only characteristic of individuals of a species. Again, a color, in association with other colors, is different from the same color seen by itself. It has a distinct and peculiar power upon the retina dependent on its association. Consequently, the color of any object is not more dependent upon the nature of the object itself, and the eye beholding it, than on the color of the objects near it ; in this respect also, therefore, it is no characteristic.

Invention is in landscape nothing more than appropriate recollection—(good in proportion as it is distinct.) Then let the details of the foreground be separately studied, especially those plants which appear peculiar to the place : if any one, however unimportant, occurs there, which occurs not elsewhere, it should occupy a prominent position ; for the other details, the highest examples of the ideal forms* or charac-

---

* "Talk of improving nature when it *is* nature—Nonsense."—*E. V. Rippingille.* I have not yet spoken of the difference—even in what we commonly call Nature—between imperfect and ideal form : the study of this difficult question must, of course, be deferred until we have examined the nature of our impressions of beauty ; but it may not be out of place here to hint at the want of care in many of our artists to distinguish between the real work of nature and the diseased results of man's interference

ters which he requires are to be selected by the
artist from his former studies, or fresh studies
made expressly for the purpose, leaving as little
as possible—beyond their connection and arrangement—to mere imagination. When his
picture is perfectly realized in all its parts, let
him dash as much of it out as he likes ; throw,
if he will, mist around it, darkness, or dazzling

---

with her. Many of the works of our greatest artists have
for their subjects nothing but hacked and hewn remnants
of farm-yard vegetation, branded root and branch, from
their birth, by the prong and the pruning-hook ; and the
feelings once accustomed to take pleasure in such abor-
tions, can scarcely become perceptive of forms truly ideal.
I have just said that young painters should go to nature
trustingly,—rejecting nothing, and selecting nothing :
so they should ; but they must be careful that it *is*
nature to whom they go—nature in her liberty—not as
servant-of-all-work in the hands of the agriculturist, nor
stiffened into court-dress by the landscape gardener. It
must be the pure, wild volition and energy of the creation which they follow—not subdued to the furrow, and
cicatrized to the pollard—not persuaded into proprieties,
nor pampered into diseases. Let them work by the tor-
rent side, and in the forest shadows ; not by purling
brooks and under " tonsile shades." It is impossible to
enter here into discussion of what man can or cannot do,
by assisting natural operations : it is an intricate question:
nor can I, without anticipating what I shall have hereafter
to advance, show how or why it happens that the race-
horse is *not* the artist's ideal of a horse, nor a prize tulip
his ideal of a flower ; but so it is. As far as the painter

and confused light—whatever, in fact, impetuous feeling or vigorous imagination may dictate or desire ; the forms, once so laboriously realized, will come out, whenever they do occur, with a startling and impressive truth, which the uncertainty in which they are veiled will enhance rather than diminish, and the imagination strengthened by discipline, and fed with truth,

---

is concerned, man never touches nature but to spoil ; he operates on her as a barber would on the Apollo ; and if he sometimes increases some particular power or excellence,—strength or agility in the animal, tallness, or fruitfulness, or solidity in the tree,—he invariably loses that *balance* of good qualities which is the chief sign of perfect specific form ; above all, he destroys the appearance of free *volition* and *felicity*, which, as I shall show hereafter, is one of the essential characters of organic beauty.   Until, however, I can enter into the discussion of the nature of beauty, the only advice I can safely give the young painter, is to keep clear of clover-fields and parks, and to hold to the unpenetrated forest and the unfurrowed hill. There he will find that every influence is noble even when destructive—that decay itself is beautiful,—and that, in the elaborate and lovely composition of all things, if at first sight it seem less studied than the works of men, the appearance of Art is only prevented by the presence of Power.

> "Nature never did betray
> The heart that loved her : 'tis her privilege
> Through all the years of this our life to lead
> From joy to joy."

will achieve the utmost of creation that is possible to finite mind.

Our landscapes are all descriptive, not reflective; agreeable and conversational, but not
impressive nor didactic.   They have no other
foundation than

> " That vivacious versatility,
> Which many people take for want of heart.
> They err; 'tis merely what is called ' mobility;'
> A thing of temperament, and *not of art,*
> *Though seeming so from its supposed facility.*
> *   *   *   *   *
> This makes your actors, *artists*, and romancers;
> Little that's great—but much of what is clever."

Only it is to be observed that—in painters—this
vivacity is *not* always versatile. It is to be
wished that it were, but it is no such easy matter
to be versatile in painting. Shallowness of
thought insures not its variety, nor rapidity of
production its originality.

Let then every picture be painted with earnest
intention of impressing on the spectator some
elevated emotion, and exhibiting to him some
one particular, but exalted, beauty.   Let a real
subject be carefully selected, in itself suggestive
of, and replete with, this feeling and beauty.
All repetition is degradation of the art; it re-
duces it from headwork to handwork; and indicates something like a persuasion on the part of

the artist that nature is exhaustible or art perfectible ; perhaps, even, by him exhausted and perfected. All copyists are contemptible, but the copyist of himself the most so, for he has the worst original.

In the range of inorganic nature, I doubt if any object can be found more perfectly beautiful than a fresh, deep snowdrift, seen under warm light. Its curves are of inconceivable perfection and changefulness, its surface and transparency alike exquisite, its light and shade of inexhaustible variety and inimitable finish, the shadows sharp, pale, and of heavenly color, the reflected lights intense and multitudinous, and mingled with the sweet occurrences of transmitted light. No mortal hand can approach the majesty or loveliness of it, yet it is possible by care and skill at least to suggest the preciousness of its forms and intimate the nature of its light and shade; but this has never been attempted; it could not be done except by artists of a rank exceedingly high, and there is something about the feeling of snow in ordinary scenery which such men do not like. But when the same qualities are exhibited on a magnificent Alpine scale and in a position where they interfere with no feeling of life, I see not why they should be neglected, as they have hitherto been, unless that the difficulty of reconciling the brilliancy of snow with a picturesque light and shade, is so great that most good artists disguise or avoid the greater part of upper Alpine scenery, and hint at the glacier so slightly, that they do not feel the necessity of careful study of its forms. Habits of exaggeration increase the evil: I have seen a sketch from nature, by one of the most able of our landscape painters, in which a cloud had been mistaken for a snowy summit, and the hint thus taken exaggerated, as was likely, into an enormous mass of impossible height, and unintelligent form, when the mountain itself, for which the cloud had been mistaken, though subtending an angle of about eighteen or twenty degrees, instead of the fifty attributed to it, was of a form so exquisite that it might have been a profitable lesson truly studied to Phidias. Nothing but failure can result from such methods of sketching, nor have I ever seen a single instance of an earnest study of snowy mountains by any one. Hence, wherever they are introduced, their drawing is utterly unintelligent, the forms being those of white rocks, or of rocks lightly powdered with snow, showing sufficiently that not only the painters have never studied the mountain carefully from below, but that they have never climbed into the snowy region.

A man accustomed to the broad, wild sea-shore, with its bright breakers, and free winds, and sounding rocks, and eternal sensation of tameless power, can scarcely but be angered when Claude bids him stand still on some paltry, chipped and chiselled quay, with porters and wheelbarrows running against him, to watch a weak, rippling, bound and barriered water, that has not strength enough in one of its waves to upset the flower-pots on the wall, or even to fling one jet of spray over the confining stone. A man accustomed to the strength and glory of God's mountains, with their soaring and radiant pinnacles, and surging sweeps of measureless distance, kingdoms in their valleys, and climates upon their crests, can scarcely but be angered when Salvator bids him stand still under some contemptible fragment of splintery crag, which an Alpine snow-wreath would smother in its first swell, with a stunted bush or two growing out of it, and a volume of manufactory smoke for a sky. A man accustomed to the grace and infinity of nature's foliage, with every vista a cathedral, and every bough a revelation, can scarcely but be angered when Poussin mocks him with a black round mass of impenetrable paint, diverging into feathers instead of leaves, and supported on a stick instead of a trunk. The fact is, there is one thing wanting in all the

doing of these men, and that is the very virtue
by which the work of human mind chiefly rises
above that of the Daguerreotype or Calotype, or
any other mechanical means that ever have been
or may be invented, Love: There is no evidence
of their ever having gone to nature with any
thirst, or received from her such emotion as could
make them, even for an instant, lose sight of
themselves; there is in them neither earnestness
nor humility; there is no simple or honest record
of any single truth; none of the plain words nor
straight efforts that men speak and make when
they once feel.

Nor is it only by the professed landscape
painters that the great verities of the material
world are betrayed: Grand as are the motives of
landscape in the works of the earlier and mightier men, there is yet in them nothing approaching to a general view nor complete rendering of
natural phenomena; not that they are to be
blamed for this; for they took out of nature that
which was fit for their purpose, and their mission
was to do no more; but we must be cautious to distinguish that imaginative abstraction of landscape
which alone we find in them, from the entire statement of truth which has been attempted by the
moderns. I have said in the chapter on symmetry
in the second volume of " Modern Painters," that
all landscape grandeur vanishes before that of

Titian and Tintoret; and this is true of whatever these two giants touched;—but they touched little. A few level flakes of chestnut foliage; a blue abstraction of hill forms from Cadore or the Euganeans; a grand mass or two of glowing ground and mighty herbage, and a few burning fields of quiet cloud were all they needed; there is evidence of Tintoret's having felt more than this, but it occurs only in secondary fragments of rock, cloud, or pine, hardly noticed among the accumulated interest of his human subject. From the window of Titian's house at Venice, the chain of the Tyrolese Alps is seen lifted in spectral power above the tufted plain of Treviso; every dawn that reddens the towers of Murano lights also a line of pyramidal fires along that colossal ridge; but there is, so far as I know, no evidence in any of the master's works of his ever having beheld, much less felt, the majesty of their burning. The dark firmament and saddened twilight of Tintoret are sufficient for their end; but the sun never plunges behind San Giorgio in Aliga without such retinue of radiant cloud, such rest of zoned light on the green lagoon, as never received image from his hand.

The modern Italians will paint every leaf of a laurel or rose-bush without the slightest feeling of their beauty or character; and without showing one spark of intellect or affection from be-

ginning to end.   Anything is better than this ;
and yet the very highest schools *do* the same
thing, or nearly so, but with totally different
motives and perceptions, and the result is divine.
On the whole, I conceive that the extremes of
good and evil lie with the finishers, and that
whatever glorious power we may admit in men
like Tintoret, whatever attractiveness of method
to Rubens, Rembrandt, or, though in far less
degree, our own Reynolds, still the thoroughly
great men are those who have done everything
thoroughly, and who, in a word, have never
despised any thing, however small, of God's
making. And this is the chief fault of our
English landscapists, that they have not the intense all-observing penetration of well-balanced
mind ; they have not, except in one or two instances, anything of that feeling which Wordsworth shows in the following lines:—

> " So fair, so sweet, withal so sensitive ;—
>   Would that the little flowers were born to live
>   Conscious of half the pleasure which they give.
>   That to this mountain daisy's self were known
>   *The beauty of its star-shaped shadow, thrown
>   On the smooth surface of this naked stone.*"

That is a little bit of good, downright, foreground painting—no mistake about it ; daisy,
and shadow, and stone texture and all. Our
painters must come to this before they have

done their duty; and yet, on the other hand,
let them beware of finishing, for the sake of finish, all over their picture. The ground is not to
be all over daisies, nor is every daisy to have its
star-shaped shadow; there is as much finish in
the right concealment of things as in the right
exhibition of them; and while I demand this
amount of specific character where nature shows
it, I demand equal fidelity to her where she conceals it.

But the painter who really loves nature will
not, on this account, give you a faded and feeble
image, which indeed may appear to you to be
right, because your feelings can detect no dis-
crepancy in its parts, but which he knows to
derive its apparent truth from a systematized
falsehood. No; he will make you understand
and feel that art *cannot* imitate nature—that
where it appears to do so, it must malign her,
and mock her. He will give you, or state to
you, such truths as are in his power, completely
and perfectly; and those which he cannot give,
he will leave to your imagination. If you are
acquainted with nature, you will know all he has
given to be true, and you will supply from your
memory and from your heart that light which
he cannot give. If you are unacquainted with
nature, seek elsewhere for whatever may happen
to satisfy your feelings; but do not ask for the

truth which you would not acknowledge and could not enjoy.

And must it ever be otherwise with painting, for otherwise it has ever been. Her subjects have been regarded as mere themes on which the artist's power is to be displayed; and that power, be it of imitation, composition, idealization, or of whatever other kind, is the chief object of the spectator's observation. It is man and his fancies, man and his trickeries, man and his inventions,—poor, paltry, weak, self-sighted man, which the connoisseur for ever seeks and worships. Among potsherds and dunghills, among drunken boors and withered beldames, through every scene of debauchery and degradation, we follow the erring artist, not to receive one wholesome lesson, not to be touched with pity, nor moved with indignation, but to watch the dexterity of the pencil, and gloat over the glittering of the hue.

I speak not only of the works of the Flemish School—I wage no war with their admirers; they may be left in peace to count the spiculæ of haystacks and the hairs of donkeys—it is also of works of real mind that I speak,—works in which there are evidences of genius and workings of power,—works which have been held up as containing all of the beautiful that art can reach or man conceive. And I assert with sorrow, that all hitherto done in landscape, by those commonly conceived its masters, has never prompted one holy thought in the minds of nations. It has begun and ended in exhibiting the dexterities of individuals, and conventionalities of systems. Filling the world with the honor of Claude and Salvator, it has never once tended to the honor of God.

Does the reader start in reading these last words, as if they were those of wild enthusiasm, —as if I were lowering the dignity of religion by supposing that its cause could be advanced by such means? His surprise proves my position. It *does* sound like wild, like absurd enthusiasm, to expect any definite moral agency in the painters of landscape; but ought it so to sound? Are the gorgeousness of the visible hue, the glory of the realized form, instruments in the artist's hand so ineffective, that they can answer no nobler purpose than the amusement of curiosity, or the engagement of idleness? Must it not be owing to gross neglect or misapplication of the means at his command, that while words and tones (means of representing nature surely less powerful than lines and colors) can kindle and purify the very inmost souls of men, the painter can only hope to entertain by his efforts at expression, and must remain forever brooding over his incommunicable thoughts?

The cause of the evil lies, I believe, deep-seated in the system of ancient landscape art; it consists, in a word, in the painter's taking upon him to modify God's works at his pleasure, casting the shadow of himself on all he sees, constituting himself arbiter where it is honor to be a disciple, and exhibiting his ingenuity by the attainment of combinations whose highest praise is that they are impossible.

Every herb and flower of the field has its specific, distinct, and perfect beauty; it has its peculiar habitation, expression, and function. The highest art is that which seizes this specific character, which developes and illustrates it, which assigns to it its proper position in the landscape, and which, by means of it, enhances and enforces the great impression which the picture is intended to convey.

Again, it does not follow that because such accurate knowledge is *necessary* to the painter that it should constitute the painter; nor that such knowledge is valuable in itself, and without reference to high ends. Every kind of knowl-edge may be sought from ignoble motives, and for ignoble ends, and in those who so possess it, it is ignoble knowledge; while the very same knowledge is in another mind an attainment of the highest dignity, and conveying the greatest blessing. This is the difference between the mere botanist's knowledge of plants, and the great poet's or painter's knowledge of them. The one notes their distinctions for the sake of swelling his herbarium ; the other, that he may render them vehicles of expression and emotion.

———◆———

CHIAROSCURO.

Go out some bright sunny day in winter, and look for a tree with a broad trunk, having rather delicate boughs hanging down on the sunny side, near the trunk. Stand four or five yards from it, with your back to the sun. You will find that the boughs between you and the trunk of the tree are very indistinct, that you confound them in places with the trunk itself, and cannot possibly trace one of them from its insertion to its extremity. But the shadows which they cast upon the trunk, you will find clear, dark, and distinct, perfectly traceable through their whole course, except when they are interrupted by the crossing boughs. And if you retire backwards, you will come to a point where you cannot see the intervening boughs at all, or only a fragment of them here and there, but

can still see their shadows perfectly plain.
Now, this may serve to show you the immense
prominence and importance of shadows where
there is anything like bright light. They are,
in fact, commonly far more conspicuous than
the thing which casts them, for being as large
as the casting object, and altogether made up
of a blackness deeper than the darkest part of
the casting object (while that object is also
broken up with positive and reflected lights),
their large, broad, unbroken spaces, tell strongly
on the eye, especially as all form is rendered
partially, often totally invisible within them,
and as they are suddenly terminated by the
sharpest lines which nature ever shows. For
no outline of objects whatsoever is so sharp as
the edge of a close shadow. Put your finger
over a piece of white paper in the sun, and observe the difference between the softness of the
outline of the finger itself and the decision of
the edge of the shadow. And note also the
excessive gloom of the latter. A piece of black
cloth, laid in the light, will not attain one-fourth
of the blackness of the paper under the shadow.

Hence shadows are in reality, when the sun
is shining, the most conspicuous thing in a
landscape, next to the highest lights. All forms
are understood and explained chiefly by their
agency: the roughness of the bark of a tree, for

instance, is not seen in the light, nor in the shade; it is only seen between the two, where the shadows of the ridges explain it. And hence, if we have to express vivid light, our very first aim must be to get the shadows sharp and visible.

The second point to which I wish at present to direct attention has reference to the *arrangement* of light and shade. It is the constant habit of nature to use both her highest lights and deepest shadows in exceedingly small quantity; always in points, never in masses. She will give a large mass of tender light in sky or water, impressive by its quantity, and a large mass of tender shadow relieved against it, in foliage, or hill, or building; but the light is always subdued if it be extensive—the shadow always feeble if it be broad. She will then fill up all the rest of her picture with middle tints and pale grays of some sort or another, and on this quiet and harmonious whole, she will touch her high lights in spots—the foam of an isolated wave—the sail of a solitary vessel—the flash of the sun from a wet roof—the gleam of a single white-washed cottage—or some such sources of local brilliancy, she will use so vividly and delicately as to throw everything else into definite shade by comparison. And then taking up the gloom, she will use the black hollows of some

overhanging bank, or the black dress of some
shaded figure, or the depth of some sunless chink
of wall or window, so sharply as to throw everything else into definite light by comparison;
thus reducing the whole mass of her picture to
a delicate middle tint, approaching, of course,
here to light, and there to gloom; but yet sharply separated from the utmost degrees either of
the one or the other. None are in the right
road to real excellence, but those who are struggling to render the simplicity, purity, and inexhaustible variety of nature's own chiaroscuro in
open, cloudless daylight, giving the expanse of
harmonious light—the speaking, decisive shadow—and the exquisite grace, tenderness, and
grandeur of aerial opposition of local color and
equally illuminated lines. No chiaroscuro is so
difficult as this; and none so noble, chaste, or
impressive. On this part of the subject, however, I must not enlarge at present. I wish now
only to speak of those great principles of chiaroscuro, which nature observes, even when she is
most working for effect—when she is playing
with thunderclouds and sunbeams, and throwing
one thing out and obscuring another, with the
most marked artistical feeling and intention;—
even then, she never forgets her great rule, to
give precisely the same quantity of deepest
shade which she does of highest light, and no

more; points of the one answering to points of the other, and both vividly conspicuous and separated from all the rest of the landscape.

----◆----

TINTORET'S MASSACRE OF THE INNOCENTS.

Of Raffaelle's treatment of the massacre of the innocents, Fuseli affirms that, " in dramatic gradation he disclosed all the mother through every image of pity and of terror." If this be so, I think the philosophical spirit has prevailed over the imaginative. The imagination never errs, it sees all that is and all the relations and bearings of it, but it would not have confused the mortal frenzy of maternal terror with various development of maternal character. Fear, rage, and agony, at their utmost pitch, sweep away all character : humanity itself would be lost in maternity, the woman would become the mere personification of animal fury or fear. For this reason all the ordinary representations of this subject are, I think, false and cold: the artist has not heard the shrieks, nor mingled with the fugitives, he has sat down in his study to twist features methodically, and philosophize over insanity. Not so Tintoret. Knowing or feeling, that the expression of the human face was in such circumstances not to be rendered, and that the effort could only end in an ugly falsehood, he denies himself all aid from the features, he feels that if he is to place himself or us in the midst of that maddened multitude, there can be no time allowed for watching expression. Still less does he depend on details of murder or ghastliness of death; there is no blood, no stabbing or cutting, but there is an awful substitute for these in the chiaroscuro. The scene is the outer vestibule of a palace, the slippery marble floor is fearfully barred across by sanguine shadows, so that our eyes seem to become bloodshot and strained with strange horror and deadly vision; a lake of life before them, like the burning scene of the doomed Moabite on the water that came by the way of Edom; a huge flight of stairs, without parapet, descends on the left; down this rush a crowd of women mixed with the murderers; the child in the arms of one has been seized by the limbs, she hurls herself over the edge, and falls head downmost, dragging the child out of the grasp by her weight;—she will be dashed dead in a second: two others are farther in flight, they reach the edge of a deep river,—the water is beat into a hollow by the force of their plunge;—close to us is the great struggle, a heap of the mothers entangled in one mortal writhe with each other and the swords, one of the murderers dashed down and crushed beneath them, the sword of another caught by the blade and dragged at by a woman's naked hand; the youngest and fairest of the women, her child just torn away from a death grasp and clasped to her breast with the grip of a steel vice, falls backwards helplessly over the heap, right on the sword points; all knit together and hurled down in one hopeless, frenzied, furious abandonment of body and soul in the effort to save. Their shrieks ring in our ears till the marble seems rending around us, but far back at the bottom of the stairs, there is something in the shadow like a heap of clothes. It is a woman, sitting quiet,—quite quiet—still as any stone, she looks down steadfastly on her dead child, laid along on the floor before her, and her hand is pressed softly upon her brow.

All the parts of a noble work must be separately imperfect; each must imply, and ask for all the rest, and the glory of every one of them must consist in its relation to the rest, neither while so much as one is wanting can any be right. And it is evidently impossible to conceive in each separate feature, a certain want or wrongness which can only be corrected by the other features of the picture (not by one or two merely, but by all), unless together with the want, we conceive also of what is wanted, that is of all the rest of the work or picture. Hence Fuseli:—

"Second thoughts are admissible in painting and poetry only as dressers of the first conception; no great idea was ever formed in fragments."

THE BAPTISM OF CHRIST.

Tintoret has thrown into it his utmost strength, and it becomes noble in his hands by his most singularly imaginative expression, not only of the immediate fact, but of the whole train of thought of which it is suggestive; and by his considering the baptism not only as the submission of Christ to the fulfilment of all righteousness, but as the opening of the earthly struggle with the prince of the power of the air, which instantly beginning in the temptation, ended only on the cross.

The river flows fiercely under the shadow of a great rock. From its opposite shore, thickets of close, gloomy foliage rise against the rolling chasm of heaven, through which breaks the brightness of the descending Spirit. Across these, dividing them asunder, is stretched a horizontal floor of flaky cloud, on which stand hosts of heaven. Christ kneels upon the water, and does not sink; the figure of St. John is indistinct, but close beside his raised right arm there is a spectre in the black shade; the fiend, harpy-shaped, hardly seen, glares down upon Christ with eyes of fire, waiting his time. Beneath this figure there comes out of the mist a dark hand, the arm unseen, extended to a net in the river, the spars of which are in the shape of a cross. Behind this the roots and under stems of the trees are cut away by the cloud, and beneath it, and through them, is seen a vision of wild, melancholy, boundless light, the sweep of the desert, and the figure of Christ is seen therein alone, with his arms lifted as in supplication or ecstacy, borne of the Spirit into the wilderness to be tempted of the devil.

THE IDEAL OF HUMANITY.

The right ideal is to be reached, we have asserted, only by the banishment of the immediate signs of sin upon the countenance and body. How, therefore, are the signs of sin to be known and separated?

No intellectual operation is here of any avail. There is not any reasoning by which the evi-

dences of depravity are to be traced in move-
ments of muscle or forms of feature; there is not
any knowledge, nor experience, nor diligence of
comparison that can be of avail. Here, as
throughout the operation of the theoretic
faculty, the perception is altogether moral, an
instinctive love and clinging to the lines of light.
Nothing but love can read the letters, nothing
but sympathy catch the sound, there is no pure
passion that can be understood or painted except by pureness of heart; the foul or blunt feeling will see itself in everything, and set down
blasphemies.

God has employed certain colors in His creation as the unvarying accompaniment of all that
is purest, most innocent, and most precious;
while for things precious only in material uses,
or dangerous, common colors are reserved. Consider for a little while what sort of a world it
would be if all flowers were gray, all leaves black,
and the sky *brown.* Observe how constantly innocent things are bright in color; look at a dove's
neck, and compare it with the gray back of a
viper; I have often heard talk of brilliantly colored serpents; and I suppose there are such,—
as there are gay poisons, like the foxglove and
kalmia—types of deceit; but all the venomous
serpents I have really *seen* are gray, brick-red,

or brown, variously mottled; and the most awful
serpent I have seen, the Egyptian asp, is precisely of the color of gravel, or only a little
grayer. So, again, the crocodile and alligator
are gray, but the innocent lizard green and
beautiful. I do not mean that the rule is invariable, otherwise it would be more convincing
than the lessons of the natural universe are intended ever to be; there are beautiful colors on
the leopard and tiger, and in the berries of the
nightshade; and there is nothing very notable in
brilliancy of color either in sheep or cattle
(though, by the way, the velvet of a brown bull's
hide in the sun, or the tawny white of the Italian oxen, is, to my mind, lovelier than any leopard's or tiger's skin): but take a wider view of
nature, and compare generally rainbows, sunrises,
roses, violets, butterflies, birds, goldfish, rubies,
opals, and corals, with alligators, hippopotami,
lions, wolves, bears, swine, sharks, slugs, bones,
fungi, fogs, and corrupting, stinging, destroying
things in general, and you will feel then how the
question stands between the colorists and
chiaroscurists,—which of them have nature and
life on their side, and which have sin and death.

We have been speaking hitherto of what is
constant and necessary in nature, of the ordinary effects of daylight on ordinary colors, and

we repeat again, that no gorgeousness of the pallet can reach even these. But it is a widely different thing when nature herself takes a coloring fit, and does something extraordinary, something really to exhibit her power. She has a thousand ways and means of rising above herself, but incomparably the noblest manifestations of her capability of color are in the sunsets among the high clouds. I speak especially of the moment before the sun sinks, when his light turns pure rose-color, and when this light falls upon a zenith covered with countless cloudforms of inconceivable delicacy, threads and flakes of vapor, which would in common daylight be pure snow white, and which give therefore fair field to the tone of light. There is then no limit to the multitude, and no check to the intensity of the hues assumed. The whole sky from the zenith to the horizon becomes one molten, mantling sea of color and fire; every black bar turns into massy gold, every ripple and wave into unsullied, shadowless crimson, and purple, and scarlet, and colors for which there are no words in language, and no ideas in the mind,—things which can only be conceived while they are visible,—the intense hollow blue of the upper sky melting through it all,—showing here deep, and pure, and lightless, there, modulated by the filmy, formless body of the transparent vapor, till it is lost imperceptibly in its crimson and gold.

The concurrence of circumstances necessary to produce the sunsets of which I speak does not take place above five or six times in a summer, and then only for a space of from five to ten minutes, just as the sun reaches the horizon. Considering how seldom people think of looking for sunset at all, and how seldom, if they do, they are in a position from which it can be fully seen, the chances that their attention should be awake, and their position favorable, during these few flying instants of the year, is almost as nothing. What can the citizen, who can see only the red light on the canvas of the wagon at the end of the street, and the crimson color of the bricks of his neighbor's chimney, know of the flood of fire which deluges the sky from the horizon to the zenith? What can even the quiet inhabitant of the English lowlands, whose scene for the manifestation of the fire of heaven is limited to the tops of hayricks, and the rooks' nests in the old elm-trees, know of the mighty passages of splendor which are tossed from Alp to Alp over the azure of a thousand miles of champaign? Even granting the constant vigor of observation, and supposing the possession of such impossible knowledge, it needs but a moment's reflection to prove how incapable the memory is of retaining for any time the distinct image of the sources even of its most vivid impressions. What recollection have we of the sunsets which delighted us last year? We may know that they were magnificent, or glowing, but no distinct image of color or form is retained —nothing of whose *degree* (for the great difficulty with the memory is to retain, not facts, but *degrees* of fact) we could be so certain as to say of anything now presented to us, that it is like it. If we did say so, we should be wrong; for we may be quite certain that the energy of an impression fades from the memory, and becomes more and more indistinct every day; and thus we compare a faded and indistinct image with the decision and certainty of one present to the senses.

Recognition is no proof of real and intrinsic resemblance. We recognise our books by their bindings, though the true and essential characteristics lie inside. A man is known to his dog by the smell—to his tailor by the coat—to his friend by the smile: each of these knows him, but how little, or how much, depends on the dignity of the intelligence. That which is truly and indeed characteristic of the man, is known only to God.

One portrait of a man may possess exact ac-

curacy of feature, and no atom of expression; it
may be, to use the ordinary terms of admiration
bestowed on such portraits by those whom they
please, " as like as it can stare." Everybody,
down to his cat, would know this. Another por
trait may have neglected or misrepresented the
features, but may have given the flash of the eye,
and the peculiar radiance of the lip, seen on him
only in his hours of highest mental excitement.
None but his friends would know this. Another
may have given none of his ordinary expressions,
but one which he wore in the most excited instant of his life, when all his secret passions and
all his highest powers were brought into play at
once. None but those who had then seen him
might recognise *this* as like. But which would
be the most truthful portrait of the *man?* The
first gives the accidents of body, the sport of
climate, and food, and time—which corruption
inhabits, and the worm waits for. The second
gives the stamp of the soul on the flesh; but it
is the soul seen in the emotions which it shares
with many—which may not be characteristic of
its essence—the results of habit, and education,
and accident; a gloze, whether purposely worn,
or unconsciously assumed, perhaps totally contrary to all that is rooted and real in the mind
that it conceals. The third has caught the
trace of all that was most hidden and most

mighty, when all hypocrisy, and all habit, and
all petty and passing emotion—the ice, and the
bank and the foam of the immortal river—were
shivered and broken, and swallowed up in the
awakening of its inward strength; when the call
and claim of some divine motive had brought
into visible being those latent forces and feelings which the spirit's own volition could not
summon, nor its consciousness comprehend;
which God only knew, and God only could
awaken,—the depth and the mystery of its peculiar and separating attributes.

In a man, to be short-legged or long-nosed, or
anything else of accidental quality, does not distinguish him from other short-legged or long-
nosed animals; but the important truths respecting a man are, first, the marked development of
that distinctive organization which separates
him as man from other animals, and secondly,
that group of qualities which distinguish the individual from all other men, which make him
Paul or Judas, Newton or Shakspeare.

That habit of the old and great painters of
introducing portrait into all their highest works,
I look to, not as error in them, but as the very
source and root of their superiority in all things,
for they were too great and too humble not to

see in every face about them that which was above them, and which no fancies of theirs could match nor take place of; wherefore we find the custom of portraiture constant with them, both portraiture of study and for purposes of analysis, as with Leonardo; and actual, professed, serviceable, hard-working portraiture of the men of their time, as with Raffaelle, and Titian, and Tintoret.

There is not any greater sign of the utter want of vitality and hopefulness in the schools of the present day than that unhappy prettiness and sameness under which they mask, or rather for which they barter, in their lentile thirst, all the birthright and power of nature, which prettiness, wrought out and spun fine in the study, out of empty heads, till it hardly betters the blocks on which dresses and hair are tried in barbers' windows and milliners' books, cannot but be revolting to any man who has his eyes, even in a measure, open to the divinity of the immortal seal on the common features that he meets in the highways and hedges hourly and momentarily, outreaching all efforts of conception as all power of realization, were it Raffaelle's three times over, even when the glory of the wedding garment is not there.

Public taste, I believe, as far as it is the encourager and supporter of art, has been the same in all ages,—a fitful and vacillating current of vague impression, perpetually liable to change, subject to epidemic desires, and agitated by infectious passion, the slave of fashion, and the fool of fancy, but yet always distinguishing with singular clearsightedness, between that which is best and that which is worst of the particular class of food which its morbid appetite may call for; never failing to distinguish that which is produced by intellect, from that which is not, though it may be intellect degraded by ministering to its misguided will. Public taste may thus degrade a race of men capable of the highest efforts in art into the portrait painters of ephemeral fashions, but it will yet not fail of discovering who among these portrait painters is the man of the most mind. It will separate the man who would have become Buonaroti from the man who would have become Bandinelli, though it will employ both in painting curls, and feathers, and bracelets. Hence, generally speaking, there is no *comparative* injustice done, no false elevation of the fool above the man of mind, provided only that the man of mind will condescend to supply the particular article which the public chooses to want. Of course a thousand modifying circumstances interfere with the action of the general rule; but, taking one case with another, we shall very constantly find the price which the picture commands in the market a pretty fair standard of the artist's rank of intellect. The press, therefore, and all who pretend to lead the public taste, have not so much to direct the multitude whom to go to, as what to ask for. Their business is not to tell us which is our best painter, but to tell us whether we are making our best painter do his best.

Now none are capable of doing this, but those whose principles of judgment are based both on thorough *practical* knowledge of art, and on broad general views of what is true and right, without reference to what has been done at one time or another, or in one school or another. Nothing can be more perilous to the cause of art, than the constant ringing in our painters' ears of the names of great predecessors, as their examples or masters.

One of the most morbid symptoms of the general taste of the present day, is a too great fondness for unfinished works. Brilliancy and rapidity of execution are everywhere sought as the highest good, and so that a picture be cleverly handled as far as it is carried, little regard is paid to its imperfection as a whole. Hence some artists are permitted, and others com-

lieved gods of the elements: in Dante and the mediævals, it formed the faithfully believed angelic presence: in the modern, it creates no perfect form, does not apprehend distinctly any Divine being or operation; but only a dim, slightly credited animation in the natural object, accompanied with great interest and affection for it. This feeling is quite universal with us, only varying in depth according to the greatness of the heart that holds it; and in Scott, being more than usually intense, and accompanied with infinite affection and quickness of sympathy, it enables him to conquer all tendencies to the pathetic fallacy, and, instead of making Nature anywise subordinate to himself, he makes himself subordinate to *her*—follows her lead simply —does not venture to bring his own cares and thoughts into her pure and quiet presence— paints her in her simple and universal truth, adding no result of momentary passion or fancy, and appears, therefore, at first shallower than other poets, being in reality wider and healthier. "What am I," he says continually, "that I should trouble this sincere nature with my thoughts? I happen to be feverish and depressed, and I could see a great many sad and strange things in those waves and flowers; but I have no business to see such things. Gay Greta! sweet harebells! *you* are not sad nor

merely by the quantity of pleasure it is capable
of conveying, a well-finished picture is worth to
its possessor half-a-dozen incomplete ones; and
that a perfect drawing is, simply as a source of
delight, better worth a hundred guineas than a
drawing half as finished is worth thirty. On the
other hand, the body of our artists should be
kept in mind, that by indulging the public with
rapid and unconsidered work, they are not only
depriving themselves of the benefit which each
picture ought to render to them, as a piece of
practice and study, but they are destroying the
refinement of general taste, and rendering it impossible for themselves ever to find a market for
more careful works, supposing that they were
inclined to execute them. Nor need any single
artist be afraid of setting the example, and producing labored works, at advanced prices, among
the cheap, quick drawings of the day. The
public will soon find the value of the complete
work, and will be more ready to give a large
sum for that which is inexhaustible, than a quota
of it for that which they are wearied of in a
month. The artist who never lets the price
command the picture, will soon find the picture
command the price. And it ought to be a rule
with every painter never to let a picture leave
his easel while it is yet capable of improvement,
or of having more thought put into it. The

general effect is often perfect and pleasing, and
not to be improved upon, when the details and
facts are altogether imperfect and unsatis-
factory. It may be difficult—perhaps the most
difficult task of art—to complete these details,
and not to hurt the general effect; but until the
artist can do this, his art is imperfect and his
picture unfinished. That only is a complete
picture which has both the general wholeness
and effect of nature, and the inexhaustible perfection of nature's details. And it is only in
the effort to unite these that a painter really
improves. By aiming only at details, he becomes a mechanic; by aiming only at generals,
he becomes a trickster: his fall in both cases is
sure. Two questions the artist has, therefore,
to ask himself,—first, " Is my whole right?"
Secondly, "Can my details be added to? Is
there a single space in the picture where I can
crowd in another thought ? Is there a curve in
it which I can modulate—a line which I can
graduate—a vacancy I can fill ? Is there a single spot which the eye, by any peering or prying,
can fathom or exhaust? If so, my picture is
imperfect, and if, in modulating the line or filling the vacancy, I hurt the general effect, my
art is imperfect."

But on the other hand, though incomplete
pictures ought neither to be produced nor pur-

chased, *careful and real sketches* ought to be valued much more highly than they are.

If I stand by a picture in the Academy, and hear twenty persons in succession admiring some paltry piece of mechanism or imitation in the lining of a cloak, or the satin of a slipper, it is absurd to tell me that they reprobate collectively what they admire individually: or, if they pass with apathy by a piece of the most noble conception or most perfect truth, because it has in it no tricks of the brush nor grimace of expression, it is absurd to tell me that they collectively respect what they separately scorn, or that the feelings and knowledge of such judges, by any length of time or comparison of ideas, could come to any right conclusion with respect to what is really high in art. The question is not decided by them, but for them;—decided at first by few: by fewer in proportion as the merits of the work are of a higher order. From these few the decision is communicated to the number next below them in rank of mind, and by these again to a wider and lower circle; each rank being so far cognizant of the superiority of that above it, as to receive its decision with respect; until, in process of time, the right and consistent opinion is communicated to all, and held by all as a matter of faith, the more positively in proportion as the grounds of it are less perceived.*

---

* There are, however, a thousand modifying circumstances which render this process sometimes unnecessary, —sometimes rapid and certain—sometimes impossible. It is unnecessary in rhetoric and the drama, because the multitude is the only proper judge of those arts whose end is to move the multitude (though more is necessary to a fine play than is essentially dramatic, and it is only of the dramatic part that the multitude are cognizant). It is unnecessary, when, united with the higher qualities of a work, there are appeals to universal passion, to all the faculties and feelings which are general in man as an animal. The popularity is then as sudden as it is well grounded,—it is hearty and honest in every mind, but it is based in every mind on a different species of excellence. Such will often be the case with the noblest works of literature. Take Don Quixote for example. The lowest mind would find in it perpetual and brutal amusement in the misfortunes of the knight, and perpetual pleasure in sympathy with the squire. A mind of average feeling would perceive the satirical meaning and force of the book, would appreciate its wit, its elegance, and its truth. But only elevated and peculiar minds discover, in addition to all this, the full moral beauty of the love and truth which are the constant associates of all that is even most weak and erring in the character of its hero, and pass over the rude adventure and scurrile jest in haste— perhaps in pain, to penetrate beneath the rusty corslet, and catch from the wandering glance, the evidence and expression of fortitude, self-devotion, and universal love. So again, with the works of Scott and Byron; popularity was as instant as it was deserved, because there is in them

But when this process has taken place, and
the work has become sanctified by time in the
minds of men, it is impossible that any new work
of equal merit can be impartially compared with
it, except by minds not only educated and generally capable of appreciating merit, but strong
enough to shake off the weight of prejudice and

---

an appeal to those passions which are universal in all
men, as well as an expression of such thoughts as can be
received only by the few. But they are admired by the
majority of their advocates for the weakest parts of their
works, as a popular preacher by the majority of his congregation for the worst part of his sermon.

The process is rapid and certain, when, though there
may be little to catch the multitude at once, there is
much which they can enjoy when their attention is au-
thoritatively directed to it. So rests the reputation of
Shakspeare. No ordinary mind can comprehend wherein
his undisputed superiority consists, but there is yet quite
as much to amuse, thrill, or excite,—quite as much of
what is in the strict sense of the word, dramatic, in his
works as in any one else's. They were received, therefore, when first written, with average approval as works
of common merit: but when the high decision was made,
and the circle spread, the public took up the hue and cry
conscientiously enough. Let them have daggers, ghosts,
clowns, and kings, and with such real and definite sources
of enjoyment, they will take the additional trouble to
learn half a dozen quotations, without understanding
them, and admit the superiority of Shakspeare without
further demur.

association, which invariably incline them to
the older favorite.

There is sublimity and power in every field of
nature from the pole to the line ; and though
the painters of one country are often better and
greater, universally, than those of another, this is
less because the subjects of art are wanting anywhere, than because one country or one age breeds
mighty and thinking men, and another none.

The world does, indeed, succeed—oftener
than is, perhaps, altogether well for the world—
in making Yes mean No, and No mean Yes.
But the world has never succeeded, nor ever will,
in making itself delight in black clouds more
than in blue sky, or love the dark earth better
than the rose that grows from it. Happily for
mankind, beauty and ugliness are as positive in
their nature as physical pain and pleasure, as
light and darkness, or as life and death ; and,
though they may be denied or misunderstood in
many fantastic ways, the most subtle reasoner
will at least find that color and sweetness are
still attractive to him, and that no logic will enable him to think the rainbow sombre, or the
violet scentless. But the theory that beauty
was merely a result of custom was very common
in Johnson's time. Goldsmith has, I think, expressed it with more force and wit than any

other writer, in various passages of the Citizen
of the World. And it was, indeed, a curious
retribution of the folly of the world of art, which
for some three centuries had given itself reck-
lessly to the pursuit of beauty, that at last it
should be led to deny the very existence of what
it had so morbidly and passionately sought. It
was as if a child should leave its home to pursue
the rainbow, and then, breathless and hopeless,
declare that it did not exist. Nor is the lesson
less useful which may be gained in observing the
adoption of such a theory by Reynolds himself.
It shows how completely an artist may be unconscious of the principles of his own work, and
how he may be led by instinct to *do* all that is
right, while he is misled by false logic to *say* all
that is wrong. For nearly every word that Reynolds wrote was contrary to his own practice ;
he seems to have been born to teach all error by
his precept, and all excellence by his example ;
he enforced with his lips generalization and idealism, while with his pencil he was tracing the
patterns of the dresses of the belles of his day ;
he exhorted his pupils to attend only to the invariable, while he himself was occupied in distinguishing every variation of womanly temper ; and
he denied the existence of the beautiful, at the
same instant that he arrested it as it passed, and
perpetuated it for ever.

The knowing of rules and the exertion of judgment have a tendency to check and confuse the fancy in its flow; so that it will follow, that, in exact proportion as a master knows anything about rules of right and wrong, he is likely to be uninventive; and in exact proportion, as he holds higher rank and has nobler inventive power, he will know less of rules; not despising them, but simply feeling that between him and them there is nothing in common,—that dreams cannot be ruled—that as they come so they must be caught, and they cannot be caught in any other shape than that they come in; and that he might as well attempt to rule a rainbow into rectitude, or cut notches in a moth's wings to hold it by, as in any wise attempt to modify, by rule, the forms of the involuntary vision.

And this, which by reason we have thus anticipated, is in reality universally so. There is no exception. The great men never know how or why they do things. They have no rules; cannot comprehend the nature of rules;—do not, usually, even know, in what they do, what is best or what is worst: to them it is all the same; something they cannot help saying or doing,— one piece of it as good as another, and none of it (it seems to *them*) worth much. The moment any man begins to talk about rules, in whatsoever art, you may know him for a second-rate man;

and, if he talks about them *much*, he is a third-rate, or not an artist at all. To *this* rule there is no exception in any art ; but it is perhaps better to be illustrated in the art of music than in that of painting. I fell by chance the other day upon a work of De Stendhal's, " Vies de Haydn, de Mozart, et de Metastase," fuller of common sense than any book I ever read on the arts ; though I see, by the slight references a de occasionally to painting, that the author's knowledge therein is warped and limited by the elements of general teaching in the schools around him ; and I have not yet, therefore, looked at what he has separately written on painting. But one or two passages out of this book on music are closely to our present purpose.

"Counterpoint is related to mathematics: a fool, with patience, becomes a respectable savant in that ; but for the part of genius, melody, it has no rules. No art is so utterly deprived of precepts for the production of the beautiful. So much the better for it and for us. Cimarosa, when first at Prague his air was executed, Pria che spunti in ciel l'Aurora, never heard the pedants say to him, ' Your air is fine, because you have followed such and such a rule established by Pergolese in such an one of his airs ; but it would be finer still if you had conformed

yourself to such another rule from which Gal-
luppi never deviated.'"

Yes: "so much the better for it, and for us ;"
but I trust the time will soon come when melody
in painting will be understood, no less than in
music, and when people will find that, there also,
the great melodists have no rules, and cannot
have any, and that there are in this, as in sound,
"no precepts for the production of the beautiful."

Again. "Behold, my friend, an example of
that simple way of answering which embarrasses
much. One asked him (Haydn) the *reason* for
a harmony—for a passage's being assigned to one
instrument rather than another ; but all he ever
answered was, 'I have done it, because it does
well.'" Farther on, De Stendhal relates an anecdote of Haydn; I believe one well known,
but so much to our purpose that I repeat it.
Haydn had agreed to give some lessons in
counterpoint to an English nobleman. "'For
our first lesson,' said the pupil, already learned
in the art—drawing at the same time a quatuor
of Haydn's from his pocket,—'for our first lesson, may we examine this quatuor ; and will you
tell me the reasons of certain modulations, which
I cannot entirely approve, because they are contrary to the principles ?' Haydn, a little surprised, declared himself ready to answer. The

nobleman began ; and at the very first measures
found matter for objection. Haydn, *who invented habitually*, and who was the contrary of a
pedant, found himself much embarrassed, and
answered always, 'I have done that because it
has a good effect. I have put that passage there
because it does well.' The Englishman, who
judged that these answers proved nothing, re-
commenced his proofs, and demonstrated to
him, by very good reasons, that this quatuor was
good for nothing. 'But, my lord, arrange this
quatuor then to your fancy,—play it so, and you
will see which of the two ways is the best.'
'But why is yours the best which is contrary to
the rules?' 'Because it is the pleasantest.'
The nobleman replied. Haydn at last lost patience, and said, 'I see, my lord, it is you who
have the goodness to give lessons to me, and
truly I am forced to confess to you that I do not
deserve the honor.' The partizan of the rules
departed, still astonished that in following the
rules to the letter one cannot infallibly produce
a 'Matrimonio Segreto.'"

This anecdote, whether in all points true or
not, is in its tendency most instructive, except
only in that it makes *one* false inference or admission, namely, that a good composition can
be *contrary* to the rules. It may be contrary to
certain principles, supposed in ignorance to be

general ; but every great composition is in perfect harmony with all true rules, and involves thousands too delicate for ear, or eye, or thought, to trace ; still it is possible to reason, with infinite pleasure and profit, about these principles, when the thing is once done ; only, all our reasoning will not enable any one to do another thing like it, because all reasoning falls infinitely short of the divine instinct. Thus we may reason wisely over the way a bee builds its comb, and be profited by finding out certain things about the angles of it. But the bee knows nothing about those matters. It builds its comb in a far more inevitable way. And, from a bee to Paul Veronese, all master-workers work with this awful, this inspired unconsciousness.

I said just now that there was no exception to *this* law, that the great men never knew how or why they did things. It is, of course, only with caution that such a broad statement should be made ; but I have seen much of different kinds of artists, and I have always found the knowledge of, and attention to, rules so *accurately* in the inverse ratio to the power of the painter, that I have myself no doubt that the law is constant, and that men's smallness may be trigonometrically estimated by the attention which, in their work, they pay to principles, especially principles of composition. The general way in which the great men speak is of " *trying* to do" this or that, just as a child would tell of something he had seen and could not utter.

And this is the reason for the somewhat singular, but very palpable truth that the Chinese, and Indians, and other semi-civilized nations, can color better than we do, and that an Indian shawl or Chinese vase are still, in invention of color, inimitable by us. It is their glorious ignorance of all rules that does it ; the pure and true instincts have play, and do their work,—instincts so subtle, that the least warping or compression breaks or blunts them ; and the moment we begin teaching people any rules about color, and make them do this or that, we crush the instinct generally for ever. Hence, hitherto, it has been an actual necessity, in order to obtain power of coloring, that a nation should be half savage : everybody could color in the twelfth and thirteenth centuries ; but we were ruled and legalized into gray in the fifteenth ;—only a little salt simplicity of their sea natures at Venice still keeping their precious, shell-fishy purpleness and power ; and now that is gone ; and nobody can color anywhere, except the Hindoos and Chinese ; but that need not be so, and will not be so long ; for, in a little while, people will find out their mistake, and give up talking about

rules of color, and then everybody will color
again, as easily as they now talk.

Such, then, being the generally passive or instinctive character of right invention, it may be
asked how these unmanageable instincts are to
be rendered practically serviceable in historical
or poetical painting,—especially historical, in
which between men who, like Horace Vernet,
David, or Domenico Tintoret, would employ
themselves in painting, more or less graphically,
the outward verities of passing events—battles,
councils, etc.,—of their day (who, supposing
them to work worthily of their mission, would
become, properly so called, historical or narrative
painters) ; and men who sought, in scenes of
perhaps less outward importance, " noble grounds
for noble emotion ;"—who would be, in a certain
separate sense, *poetical* painters ; some of them
taking for subjects events which had actually
happened, and others themes from the poets ;
or, better still, becoming poets themselves in the
entire sense, and inventing the story as they
painted it.   Painting seems to me only just to be
beginning, in this sense also, to take its proper
position beside literature.

Finally, as far as I can observe, it is a constant
law that the greatest men, whether poets or historians, live entirely in their own age, and that
the greatest fruits of their work are gathered out

of their own age. Dante paints Italy in the thirteenth century ; Chaucer, England in the fourteenth ; Masaccio, Florence in the fifteenth; Tintoret, Venice in the sixteenth ;—all of them utterly regardless of anachronism and minor error of every kind, but getting always vital truth out of the vital present.

If it be said that Shakspeare wrote perfect historical plays on subjects belonging to the preceding centuries, I answer, that they *are* perfect plays just because there is no care about centuries in them, but a life which all men recognise for the human life of all time ; and this it is, not because Shakspeare sought to give universal truth, but because, painting honestly and completely from the men about him, he painted that human nature which is, indeed, constant enough, —a rogue in the fifteenth century being, *at heart*, what a rogue is in the nineteenth and was in the twelfth ; and an honest or a knightly man being, in like manner, very similar to other such at any other time. And the work of these great idealists is, therefore, always universal ; not because it is *not portrait*, but because it is *complete* portrait down to the heart, which is the same in all ages: and the work of the mean idealists is *not* universal, not because it is portrait, but because it is *half* portrait,—of the outside, the manners and the dress, not of the heart. Thus Tintoret and

Shakspeare paint, both of them, simply Venetian
and English nature as they saw it in their time,
down to the root ; and it does for *all* time ; but
as for any care to cast themselves into the particular ways and tones of thought, or custom, of
past time in their historical work, you will find
it in neither of them, nor in any other perfectly
great man that I know of.

If there had been no vital truth in their present, it is hard to say what these men could have
done.   I suppose, primarily, they would not
have existed; that they, and the matter they
have to treat of, are given together, and that the
strength of the nation and its historians correla-
tively rise and fall—Herodotus springing out of
the dust of Marathon.   It is also hard to say
how far our better general acquaintance with
minor details of past history may make us able
to turn the shadow on the imaginative dial backwards, and naturally to live, and even live
strongly if we choose, in past periods; but this
main truth will always be unshaken, that the
only historical painting deserving the name is
portraiture of our own living men and our passing times,* and that all efforts to summon up
the events of bygone periods, though often useful and touching, must come under an inferior

---

* See Edinburgh Lectures, p. 217.

class of poetical painting; nor will it, I believe, ever be much followed as their main work by the strongest men, but only by the weaker and comparatively sentimental (rather than imaginative) groups.

Suppose you have to teach two children drawing, one thoroughly clever and active-minded, the other dull and slow: and you put before them Jullien's chalk studies of heads—*études à deux crayons*—and desire them to be copied. The dull child will slowly do your bidding, blacken his paper and rub it white again, and patiently and painfully, in the course of three or four years, attain to the performance of a chalk-head, not much worse than his original, but still of less value than the paper it is drawn upon. But the clever child will not, or will only by force, consent to this discipline. He finds other means of expressing himself with his pencil somehow or another; and presently you find his paper covered with sketches of his grandfather and grandmother, and uncles, and cousins,—sketches of the room, and the house, and the cat, and the dog, and the country outside, and everything in the world he can set his eyes on; and he gets on, and even his child's work has a value in it— a truth which makes it worth keeping; no one knows how precious, perhaps, that portrait of

his grandfather may be, if any one has but the
sense to keep it till the time when the old man
can be seen no more up the lawn, nor by the
the wood. That child is working in the middle-
age spirit—the other in the modern spirit.

But there is something still more striking in
the evils which have resulted from the modern
regardlessness of truth. Consider, for instance,
its effect on what is called historical painting.
What do you at present *mean* by historical painting? Now-a-days, it means the endeavoring, by
the power of imagination, to portray some historical event of past days. But in the middle
ages, it meant representing the acts of *their own*
days; and that is the only historical painting
worth a straw. Of all the wastes of time and
sense which modernism has invented—and they
are many—none are so ridiculous as this endeavor to represent past history. What do you
suppose our descendants will care for our imaginations of the events of former days? Suppose
the Greeks, instead of representing their own
warriors as they fought at Marathon, had left us
nothing but their imaginations of Egyptian battles; and suppose the Italians, in like manner,
instead of portraits of Can Grande and Dante,
or of Leo the Tenth and Raphael, had left us
nothing but imaginary portraits of Pericles and
Miltiades? What fools we should have thought

them! how bitterly we should have been pro-
voked with their folly! And that is precisely
what our descendants will feel towards us, so
far as our grand historical and classical schools
are concerned. What do we care, they will say,
what those 19th century people fancied about
Greek and Roman history! If they had left us
a few plain and rational sculptures and pictures
of their own battles, and their own men, in their
everyday dress, we should have thanked them.
Well, but, you will say, we *have* left them portraits of our great men, and paintings of our
great battles. Yes, you have indeed, and that
is the only historical painting that you either
have or can have; but you don't *call* that historical painting. You don't thank the men who
do it; you look down upon them and dissuade
them from it, and tell them they don't belong
to the grand schools. And yet they are the only
true historical painters, and the only men who
will produce any effect on their own generation,
or any other. Wilkie was an historical painter,
Chantrey an historical sculptor, because they
painted, or carved, the veritable things and men
they saw, not men and things as they believed
they might have been, or should have been.
But no one tells such men they are historical
painters, and they are discontented with what
they do; and poor Wilkie must needs travel to

see the grand school, and imitate the grand
school, and ruin himself.   And you have had
multitudes of other painters ruined, from the
beginning, by that grand school.   There was
Etty, naturally as good a painter as ever lived,
but no one told him what to paint, and he studied the antique, and the grand schools, and
painted dances of nymphs in red and yellow
shawls to the end of his days.   Much good may
they do you !   He is gone to the grave, a lost
mind.   There was Flaxman, another naturally
great man, with as true an eye for nature as
Raphael,—he stumbles over the blocks of the
antique statues—wanders in the dark valley of
their ruins to the end of his days.   He has left
you a few outlines of muscular men straddling
and frowning behind round shields.   Much good
may they do you !   Another lost mind.   And of
those who are lost namelessly, who have not
strength enough even to make themselves known,
the poor pale students who lie buried for ever
in the abysses of the great schools, no account
can be rendered; they are numberless.

And the wonderful thing is, that of all these
men whom you now have come to call the great
masters, there was *not one* who confessedly did
not paint his own present world, plainly and
truly.   Homer sang of what he saw; Phidias
carved what he saw; Raphael painted the men

of his own time in their own caps and mantles; and every man who has arisen to eminence in modern times has done so altogether by his working in their way, and doing the things he saw. How did Reynolds rise? Not by painting Greek women, but by painting the glorious little living ladies this, and ladies that, of his own time. How did Hogarth rise? Not by painting Athenian follies, but London follies. Who are the men who have made an impression upon you yourselves,—upon your own age? I suppose the most popular painter of the day is Landseer. Do you suppose he studied dogs and eagles out of the Elgin Marbles? And yet in the very face of these plain, incontrovertible, all-visible facts, we go on from year to year with the base system of Academy teaching, in spite of which every one of these men has risen: I say *in spite* of the entire method and aim of our art-teaching. It destroys the greater number of its pupils altogether; it hinders and paralyses the greatest. There is not a living painter whose eminence is not in spite of everything he has been taught from his youth upwards, and who, whatever his eminence may be, has not suffered much injury in the course of his victory. For observe: this love of what is called ideality or beauty in preference to truth, operates not only in making us choose the past rather than the present for our subjects, but it makes us falsify the present when we do take it for our subject. I said just now that portrait-painters were historical painters;— so they are; but not good ones, because not faithful ones. The beginning and end of modern portraiture is adulation. The painters cannot live but by flattery; we should desert them if they spoke honestly. And therefore we can have no good portraiture; for in the striving after that which is *not* in their model, they lose the inner and deeper nobleness which *is* in their model. I saw not long ago, for the first time, the portrait of a man whom I knew well,—a young man, but a religious man,—and one who had suffered much from sickness. The whole dignity of his features and person depended upon the expression of serene yet solemn purpose sustaining a feeble frame; and the painter, by way of flattering him, strengthened him, and made him athletic in body, gay in countenance, idle in gesture; and the whole power and being of the man himself were lost. And this is still more the case with our public portraits. You have a portrait, for instance, of the Duke of Wellington at the end of the North Bridge,—one of the thousand equestrian statues of Modernism,—studied from the show-riders of the amphitheatre, with their horses on their hind-legs in the sawdust. Do you suppose that was the way the Duke sat when your destinies depended on him? when the foam hung from the lips of his tired horse, and its wet limbs were dashed with the bloody slime of the battle-field, and he himself sat anxious in his quietness, grieved in his fearlessness, as he watched, scythe-stroke by scythe-stroke, the gathering in of the harvest of death? You would have done something had you thus left his image in the enduring iron, but nothing now.

But the time has at last come for all this to be put an end to; and nothing can well be more extraordinary than the way in which the men have risen who are to do it. Pupils in the same schools, receiving precisely the same instruction which for so long a time has paralysed every one of our painters,—these boys agree in disliking to copy the antique statues set before them. They copy them as they are bid, and they copy them better than any one else, they carry off prize after prize, and yet they hate their work. At last they are admitted to study from the life; they find the life very different from the antique, and say so. Their teachers tell them the antique is the best, and they mustn't copy the life. They agree among themselves that they like the life, and that copy it they will. They do copy it faithfully, and their masters forthwith declare them to be lost men. Their fellow-students hiss them whenever they enter the room. They can't help it; they join hands and tacitly resist both the hissing and the instruction. Accidentally, a few prints of the works of Giotto, a few casts from those of Ghiberti, fall into their hands, and they see in these something they never saw before—something intensely and everlastingly true. They examine farther into the matter; they discover for themselves the greater part of what I have laid before you to-night; they form themselves into a body, and enter upon that crusade which has hitherto been victorious. And which will be absolutely and triumphantly victorious. The great mistake which has hitherto prevented the public mind from fully going with them must soon be corrected. That mistake was the supposition that, instead of wishing to recur to the *principles* of the early ages, these men wished to bring back the *ignorance* of the early ages. This notion, grounded first on some hardness in their earlier works, which resulted—as it must always result —from the downright and earnest effort to paint nature as in a looking-glass, was fostered partly by the jealousy of their beaten competitors, and partly by the pure, perverse, and hopeless ignorance of the whole body of art-critics, so called, connected with the press. No notion was ever more baseless or more ridiculous.

The first and most important kind of public buildings which we are always sure to want, are schools : and I would ask you to consider very carefully, whether we may not wisely introduce some great changes in the way of school decoration. Hitherto, as far as I know, it has either been so difficult to give all the education we wanted to our lads, that we have been obliged to do it, if at all, with cheap furniture in bare walls ; or else we have considered that cheap furniture and bare walls are a proper part of the means of education ; and supposed that boys learned best when they sat on hard forms, and had nothing but blank plaster about and above them whereupon to employ their spare attention ; also, that it was as well they should be accustomed to rough and ugly conditions of things, partly by way of preparing them for the hardships of life, and partly that there might be the least possible damage done to floors and forms, in the event of their becoming, during the master's absence, the fields or instruments of battle. All this is so far well and necessary, as it relates to the training of country lads, and the first training of boys in general. But there certainly comes a period in the life of a well-educated youth, in which one of the principal elements of his education is, or ought to be, to give him refinement of habits ; and not only to

teach him the strong exercises of which his
frame is capable, but also to increase his bodily
sensibility and refinement, and show him such
small matters as the way of handling things
properly, and treating them considerately. Not
only so, but I believe the notion of fixing the
attention by keeping the room empty, is a wholly
mistaken one : I think it is just in the emptiest
room that the mind wanders most; for it gets
restless, like a bird, for want of a perch, and
casts about for any possible means of getting out
and away. And even if it be fixed, by an effort,
on the business in hand, that business becomes
itself repulsive, more than it need be, by the
vileness of its associations ; and many a study
appears dull or painful to a boy, when it is pursued on a blotted deal desk, under a wall with
nothing on it but scratches and pegs, which
would have been pursued pleasantly enough in a
curtained corner of his father's library, or at
the lattice window of his cottage. Nay, my
own belief is, that the best study of all is the
most beautiful; and that a quiet glade of forest,
or the nook of a lake shore, are worth all the
schoolrooms in Christendom, when once you are
past the multiplication table ; but be that as it
may, there is no question at all but that a time
ought to come in the life of a well trained youth,
when he can sit at a writing table without want-

ing to throw the inkstand at his neighbor; and when also he will feel more capable of certain efforts of mind with beautiful and refined forms about him than with ugly ones. When that time comes he ought to be advanced into the decorated schools; and this advance ought to be one of the important and honorable epochs of his life.

I have not time, however, to insist on the mere serviceableness to our youth of refined architectural decoration, as such; for I want you to consider the probable influence of the particular kind of decoration which I wish you to get for them, namely, historical painting. You know we have hitherto been in the habit of conveying all our historical knowledge, such as it is, by the ear only, never by the eye; all our notions of things being ostensibly derived from verbal description, not from sight. Now, I have no doubt that, as we grow gradually wiser—and we are doing so every day—we shall discover at last that the eye is a nobler organ than the ear; and that through the eye we must, in reality, obtain, or put into form, nearly all the useful information we are to have about this world. Even as the matter stands, you will find that the knowledge which a boy is supposed to receive from verbal description is only available to him so far as in any underhand way he gets a sight of the thing you are talking about. I remember well that, for many years of my life, the only notion I had of the look of a Greek knight was complicated between recollection of a small engraving in my pocket Pope's Homer, and reverent study of the Horse-Guards. And though I believe that most boys collect their ideas from more varied sources, and arrange them more carefully than I did; still, whatever sources they seek must always be ocular: if they are clever boys, they will go and look at the Greek vases and sculptures in the British Museum, and at the weapons in our armories— they will see what real armor is like in lustre, and what Greek armor was like in form, and so put a fairly true image together, but still not, in ordinary cases, a very living or interesting one. Now, the use of your decorative painting would be, in myriads of ways, to animate their history for them, and to put the living aspect of past things before their eyes as faithfully as intelligent invention can; so that the master shall have nothing to do but once to point to the school-room walls, and for ever afterwards the meaning of any word would be fixed in a boy's mind in the best possible way. Is it a question of classical dress—what a tunic was like, or a chlamys, or a peplus? At this day, you have to point to some vile woodcut, in the middle of a dictionary page, representing the thing hung upon a stick; but then, you would point to a hundred figures, wearing the actual dress, in its fiery colors, in all the actions of various stateliness or strength; you would understand at once how it fell round the people's limbs as they stood, how it drifted from their shoulders as they went, how it veiled their faces as they wept, how it covered their heads in the day of battle. *Now*, if you want to see what a weapon is like, you refer, in like manner, to a numbered page, in which there are spearheads in rows, and sword-hilts in symmetrical groups; and gradually the boy gets a dim mathematical notion how one scymitar is hooked to the right and another to the left, and one javelin has a knob to it and another none: while one glance at your good picture would show him,—and the first rainy afternoon in the school-room would for ever fix in his mind,—the look of the sword and spear as they fell or flew; and how they pierced, or bent, or shattered— how men wielded them, and how men died by them. But far more than all this, is it a question not of clothes or weapons, but of men? how can we sufficiently estimate the effect on the mind of a noble youth, at the time when the world opens to him, of having faithful and touching representations put before him of the acts and presences of great men—how many a resolution,

which would alter and exalt the whole course of
his after-life, might be formed, when in some
dreamy twilight he met, through his own tears,
the fixed eyes of those shadows of the great
dead, unescapable and calm, piercing to his soul;
or fancied that their lips moved in dread reproof
or soundless exhortation. And if but for one
out of many this were true—if yet, in a few, you
could be sure that such influence had indeed
changed their thoughts and destinies, and turned
the eager and reckless youth, who would have
cast away his energies on the race-horse or the
gambling-table, to that noble life-race, that holy
life-hazard, which should win all glory to himself and all good to his country—would not that,
to some purpose, be "political economy of art"?

And observe, there could be no monotony, no
exhaustibleness, in the scenes required to be
thus portrayed. Even if there were, and you
wanted for every school in the kingdom, one
death of Leonidas; one battle of Marathon; one
death of Cleobis and Bito; there need not therefore be more monotony in your art than there
was in the repetition of a given cycle of subjects
by the religious painters of Italy. But we ought
not to admit a cycle at all. For though we had
as many great schools as we have great cities
(one day I hope we *shall* have), centuries of
painting would not exhaust, in all the number of

them, the noble and pathetic subjects which might be chosen from the history of even one noble nation. But, besides this, you will not, in a little while, limit your youths' studies to so narrow fields as you do now. There will come a time—I am sure of it—when it will be found that the same practical results, both in mental discipline, and in political philosophy, are to be attained by the accurate study of mediæval and modern as of ancient history; and that the facts of mediæval and modern history are, on the whole, the most important to us. And among these noble groups of constellated schools which I foresee arising in our England, I foresee also that there will be divided fields of thought; and that while each will give its scholars a great general idea of the world's history, such as all men should possess—each will also take upon itself, as its own special duty, the closer study of the course of events in some given place or time. It will review the rest of history, but it will exhaust its own special field of it; and found its moral and political teaching on the most perfect possible analysis of the results of human conduct in one place, and at one epoch. And then, the galleries of that school will be painted with the historical scenes belonging to the age which it has chosen for its special study.

The fact is, that the greater number of persons or societies throughout Europe, whom wealth, or chance, or inheritance has put in the possession of valuable pictures, do not know a good picture from a bad one, and have no idea in what the value of a picture really consists. The reputation of certain works is raised, partly by accident, partly by the just testimony of artists, partly and generally by the bad tastes of the public (no picture that I know of, has ever, in modern times, attained popularity, in the full sense of the term, without having some exceedingly bad qualities mingled with its good ones), and when this reputation has once been completely established, it little matters to what state the picture may be reduced: few minds are so completely devoid of imagination as to be unable to invest it with the beauties which they have heard attributed to it.

This being so, the pictures that are most valued are for the most part those by masters of established renown, which are highly or neatly finished, and of a size small enough to admit of their being placed in galleries or saloons, so as to be made subjects of ostentation, and to be easily seen by a crowd. For the support of the fame and value of such pictures, little more is necessary than that they should be kept bright, partly by cleaning, which is incipient destruction, and partly by what is called "restoring," that is, painting over, which is of course total destruction. Nearly all the gallery pictures in modern Europe have been more or less destroyed by one or the other of these operations, generally exactly in proportion to the estimation in which they are held; and as, originally, the smaller and more highly finished works of any great master are usually his worst, the contents of many of our most celebrated galleries are by this time, in reality, of very small value indeed.

On the other hand, the most precious works of any noble painter are usually those which have been done quickly, and in the heat of the first thought, on a large scale, for places where there was little likelihood of their being well seen, or for patrons from whom there was little prospect of rich remuneration. In general, the best things are done in this way, or else in the enthusiasm and pride of accomplishing some great purpose, such as painting a Cathedral or a Campo-Santo from one end to the other, especially when the time has been short, and circumstances disadvantageous. Works thus executed are of course despised on account of their quantity, as well as their frequent slightness, in the places where they exist; and they are too large to be portable, and too vast and comprehensive to be read on the spot, in the hasty temper of the present age. They are, therefore, almost universally neglected, whitewashed by custodes, shot at by soldiers, suffered to drop from the walls piecemeal into powder and rags by society in general; but, which is an advantage more than counterbalancing all this evil, they are not often "restored." What is left of them, however fragmentary, however ruinous, however obscured and defiled, is almost always *the real thing;* there are no fresh readings: and therefore the greatest treasures of art which Europe at this moment possesses are pieces of old plaster on ruinous brick walls, where the lizards burrow and bask, and which few other living creatures ever approach; and torn sheets of dim canvas, in waste corners of churches; and mildewed stains, in the shape of human figures, on the walls of dark chambers, which now and then an exploring traveller causes to be unlocked by their tottering custode, looks hastily round, and retreats from in a weary satisfaction at his accomplished duty.

Many of the pictures on the ceilings and walls of the Ducal Palace, by Paul Veronese and Tintoret, have been more or less reduced, by neglect, to this condition. Unfortunately they are not altogether without reputation, and their state has drawn the attention of the Venetian authorities and academicians. It constantly happens, that public bodies who will not pay five pounds to preserve a picture, will pay fifty to repaint it: and when I was at Venice in 1846, there were two remedial operations carrying on at one and the same time, in the two buildings which contain the pictures of greatest value in the city (as pieces of color, of greatest value in the world), curiously illustrative of this peculiarity in human nature. Buckets were set on the floor of the Scuola di San Rocco, in every shower, to catch the rain which came through the pictures of Tintoret on the ceiling; while in the Ducal Palace, those of Paul Veronese were themselves laid on the floor to be repainted; and I was myself present at the re-illumination of the breast of a white horse, with a brush, at the end of a stick five feet long, luxuriously dipped in a common house-painters' vessel of paint.

There are, indeed, some kinds of knowledge with which an artist ought to be thoroughly furnished; those, for instance, which enable him to express himself: for this knowledge relieves instead of encumbering his mind, and permits it to attend to its purposes instead of wearying itself about means. The whole mystery of manipulation and manufacture should be familiar to the painter from a child. He should know the chemistry of all colors and materials whatsoever, and should prepare all his colors himself, in a little laboratory of his own. Limiting his chemistry to this one subject, the amount of practical science necessary for it, and such accidental discoveries as might fall in his way in the course of his work, of better colors or better modes of preparing them, would be an infinite refreshment to his mind; a minor subject of interest to which it might turn when jaded with comfortless labor, or exhausted with feverish invention, and yet which would never interfere with its higher functions, when it chose to address itself to them.   Even a considerable amount of manual labor, sturdy color-grinding, and canvas-stretching, would be advantageous; though this kind of work ought to be in great part done by pupils.   For it is one of the conditions of perfect knowledge in these matters, that every great master should have a certain number of pupils, to whom he is to impart all the knowledge of materials and means which he himself possesses, as soon as possible; so that, at any rate, by the time they are fifteen years old, they may know all that he knows himself in this kind; that is to say, all that the world of artists know, and his own discoveries besides, and so never be troubled about methods any more.   Not that the knowledge even of his own particular methods is to be of purpose confined to himself and his pupils, but that necessarily it must be so in some degree; for only those who see him at work daily can understand his small and multitudinous ways of practice. These cannot verbally be explained to everybody, nor is it needful that they should, only let them be concealed from nobody who cares to see them; in which case, of course, his attendant scholars will know them best.

The art of the thirteenth century is the foundation of all art,—nor merely the foundation, but the root of it; that is to say, succeeding art is not merely built upon it, but was all comprehended in it, and is developed out of it. Passing this great century, we find three successive branches developed from it, in each of the three following centuries. The fourteenth century is pre-eminently the age of *Thought*, the fifteenth the age of *Drawing*, and the sixteenth the age of *Painting*.

Observe, first, the fourteenth century is pre-eminently the age of thought. It begins with the first words of the poem of Dante;—and all the great pictorial poems—the mighty series of works in which everything is done to relate, but nothing to imitate—belong to this century. I should only confuse you by giving you the names of marvellous artists, most of them little familiar to British ears, who adorned this century in Italy; but you will easily remember it as the age of Dante and Giotto—the age of *Thought.*

The men of the succeeding century (the fifteenth) felt that they could not rival their predecessors in invention, but might excel them in execution. Original thoughts belonging to this century are comparatively rare; even Raphael and Michael Angelo themselves borrowed all their principal ideas and plans of pictures from their predecessors; but they executed them with a precision up to that time unseen. You must understand by the word " drawing," the perfect rendering of forms, whether in sculpture or painting; and then remember the fifteenth century as the age of Leonardo, Michael Angelo, Lorenzo Ghiberti, and Raphael,—pre-eminently the age of *Drawing.*

The sixteenth century produced the four greatest *Painters,* that is to say, managers of color. that the world has seen; namely, Tintoret, Paul Veronese, Titian, and Correggio. I need not say more to justify my calling it the age of *Painting.*

POETRY.

"*Poetry is the expression of the beautiful—by words—the beautiful of the outer and the inner world; whatever is delectable to the eye or the ear, the every sense of the body and of the soul—it presides over* veras dulcedines rerum. *It implies at once a vision and a faculty, a gift and an art. A thought may be poetical, and yet not poetry; it may be a solution containing the poetical element, but waiting and wanting the precipitation of it, the crystallization of it.*"—NORTH BRITISH REVIEW.

POETRY.

I AM writing at a window which commands a
view of the head of the Lake of Geneva; and as
I look up from my paper, I see, beyond it, a blue
breadth of softly moving water, and the outline
of the mountains above Chillon, bathed in morning mist.   The first verses which naturally come
into my mind are—

> "A thousand feet in depth below
> The massy waters meet and flow;
> So far the fathom line was sent
> From Chillon's snow-white battlement."

Let us see in what manner this poetical statement is distinguished from a historical one.

It is distinguished from a truly historical
statement, first, in being simply false.   The water
under the castle of Chillon is not a thousand
feet deep, nor anything like it.*   Herein, cer-

---

* "MM. Mallet et Pictet, se trouvant sur le lac auprès
du château de Chillon, le 6 Août, 1774, plongèrent à la
profondeur de 312 pieds de un thermomètre," etc.—Saus-

tainly, these lines fulfil Reynolds's first requirement in poetry, " that it should be inattentive
to literal truth and minute exactness in detail."
In order, however, to make our comparison more
closely in other points, let us assume that what
is stated is indeed a fact, and that it was to be
recorded, first historically, and then poetically.

Historically stating it, then, we should say:
" The lake was sounded from the walls of the
castle of Chillon, and found to be a thousand
feet deep."

Now, if Reynolds be right in his idea of the
difference between history and poetry, we shall
find that Byron leaves out of this statement certain *un*necessary details, and retains only the invariable,—that is to say, the points which the
Lake of Geneva and castle of Chillon have in
common with all other lakes and castles.

Let us hear, therefore.

" A thousand feet in depth below."

"Below"? Here is, at all events, a word
added (instead of anything being taken away);
invariable, certainly in the case of lakes, but not
absolutely necessary.

" The massy waters meet and flow."

---

sure, *Voyages dans les Alpes,* chap. ii. § 33. It appears
from the next paragraph, that the thermometer was " au
fond du lac."

"Massy"! why massy? Because deep water is heavy. The word is a good word, but it is assuredly an added detail, and expresses a character, not which the Lake of Geneva has in common with all other lakes, but which it has in distinction from those which are narrow or shallow.

"Meet and flow." Why meet and flow? Partly to make up a rhyme; partly to tell us that the waters are forceful as well as massy, and changeful as well as deep. Observe, a farther addition of details, and of details more or less peculiar to the spot, or, according to Reynolds's definition, of "heavy matter, retarding the progress of the imagination."

> "So far the fathom line was sent."

Why fathom line? All lines for sounding are not fathom lines. If the lake was ever sounded from Chillon, it was probably sounded in metres, not fathoms. This is an addition of another particular detail, in which the only compliance with Reynolds's requirement is, that there is some chance of its being an inaccurate one.

> "From Chillon's snow-white battlement."

Why snow-white? Because castle battlements are not usually snow-white. This is another added detail, and a detail quite peculiar to

Chillon, and therefore exactly the most striking word in the whole passage.

" Battlement "! why battlement? Because all walls have not battlements, and the addition of the term marks the castle to be not merely a prison, but a fortress.

This is a curious result. Instead of finding, as we expected, the poetry distinguished from the history by the omission of details, we find it consist entirely in the *addition* of details; and instead of being characterized by regard only of the invariable, we find its whole power to consist in the clear expression of what is singular and particular!

The reader may pursue the investigation for himself in other instances. He will find in every case that a poetical is distinguished from a merely historical statement, not by being more vague, but more specific, and it might, therefore, at first appear that our author's comparison should be simply reversed, and that the Dutch School should be called poetical, and the Italian historical. But the term poetical does not appear very applicable to the generality of Dutch painting; and a little reflection will show us, that if the Italians represent only the invariable, they cannot be properly compared even to historians. For that which is incapable of change has no history, and records which state only the invariable need not be written, and could not be read.

It is evident, therefore, that our author has entangled himself in some grave fallacy, by introducing this idea of invariableness as forming a distinction between poetical and historical art. We must not go on with our inquiry until we have settled satisfactorily the question already suggested to us, in what the essence of poetical treatment really consists. For though, as we have seen, it certainly involves the addition of specific details, it cannot be simply that addition which turns the history into poetry. For it is perfectly possible to add any number of details to a historical statement, and to make it more prosaic with every added word. As, for instance, " The lake was sounded out of a flat-bottomed boat, near the crab-tree at the corner of the kitchen-garden, and was found to be a thousand feet nine inches deep, with a muddy bottom." It thus appears that it is not the multiplication of details which constitutes poetry; nor their subtraction which constitutes history; but that there must be something either in the nature of the details themselves, or the method of using them, which invests them with poetical power or historical propriety.

It seems to me, and may seem to the reader, strange that we should need to ask the question,

" What is poetry?" Here is a word we have been using all our lives, and, I suppose, with a very distinct idea attached to it; and when I am now called upon to give a definition of this idea, I find myself at a pause. What is more singular, I do not at present recollect hearing the question often asked, though surely it is a very natural one; and I never recollect hearing it answered, or even attempted to be answered. In general, people shelter themselves under metaphors, and while we hear poetry described as an utterance of the soul, an effusion of Divinity or voice of nature, or in other terms equally elevated and obscure, we never attain anything like a definite explanation of the character which actually distinguishes it from prose.

I come, after some embarrassment, to the conclusion, that poetry is " the suggestion, by the imagination, of noble grounds for the noble emotions." I mean, by the noble emotions, those four principal secret passions—Love, Veneration, Admiration, and Joy (this latter especially, if unselfish); and their opposites—Hatred, Indignation (or Scorn), Horror, and Grief,—this last, when unselfish, becoming Compassion. These passions in their various combinations constitute what is called "poetical feeling," when they are felt on noble grounds, that is, on great and true grounds. Indignation, for instance, is a poetical feeling, if excited by serious injury; but it is not a poetical feeling if entertained on being cheated out of a small sum of money. It is very possible the manner of the cheat may have been such as to justify considerable indignation; but the feeling is nevertheless not poetical, unless the grounds of it be large as well as just. In like manner, energetic admiration may be excited in certain minds by a display of fire-works, or a street of handsome shops; but the feeling is not poetical, because the grounds of it are false, and therefore ignoble. There is in reality nothing to deserve admiration either in the firing of packets of gunpowder, or in the display of the stocks of warehouses. But admiration excited by the budding of a flower is a poetical feeling, because it is impossible that this manifestation of spiritual power and vital beauty can ever be enough admired.

Farther, it is necessary to the existence of poetry that the grounds of these feelings should be *furnished by the imagination*. Poetical feeling, that is to say, mere noble emotion, is not poetry. It is happily inherent in all human nature deserving the name, and is found often to be purest in the least sophisticated. But the power of assembling, by *the help of the imagination*, such images as will excite these feelings, is

the power of the poet or literally of the
" Maker."*

---

* Take, for instance, the beautiful stanza in the
'' Affliction of Margaret :''

> " I look for ghosts, but none will force
>   Their way to me. 'Tis falsely said
> That ever there was intercourse
>   Between the living and the dead;
>
> For, surely then, I should have sight
> Of him I wait for, day and night,
> With love and longing infinite."

This we call Poetry, because it is invented *or made* by
the writer, entering into the mind of a supposed person.
Next, take an instance of the actual feeling truly experi-
enced and simply expressed by a real person.

" Nothing surprised me more than a woman of Argentière, whose cottage I went into to ask for milk, as I came
down from the glacier of Argentière, in the month of
March, 1764. An epidemic dysentery had prevailed in
the village, and, a few months before, had taken away
from her her father, her husband, and her brothers, so
that she was left alone, with three children in the cradle.
Her face had something noble in it, and its expression
bore the seal of a calm and profound sorrow. After having given me milk, she asked me whence I came, and
what I came there to do, so early in the year. When she
knew that I was of Geneva, she said to me, ' she could
not believe that all Protestants were lost souls; that there
were many honest people among us, and that God was
too good and too great to condemn all without distinction.'
Then, after a moment of reflection, she added, in shaking
her head, ' But, that which is very strange, is that of so

Now this power of exciting the emotions depends, of course, on the richness of the imagination, and on its choice of those images which, in combination, will be most effective, or, for the particular work to be done, most fit. And it is altogether impossible for a writer not endowed with invention to conceive what tools a true poet will make use of, or in what way he will apply them, or what unexpected results he will bring out by them; so that it is vain to say that the details of poetry ought to possess, or ever do possess, any *definite* character. Generally speaking, poetry runs into finer and more delicate details than prose; but the details are not poetical because they are more delicate, but because they are employed so as to bring out an

---

many who have gone away, none have ever returned. I,' she added, with an expression of grief, ' who have so mourned my husband and my brothers, who have never ceased to think of them, who every night conjure them with beseechings to tell me where they are, and in what state they are! Ah, surely, if they lived anywhere, they would not leave me thus! But, perhaps,' she added, ' I am not worthy of this kindness; perhaps the pure and innocent spirits of these children,' and she looked at the cradle, ' may have their presence, and the joy which is denied to *me*.' "—SAUSSURE, *Voyages dans les Alpes*, chap. xxiv.

This we do not call Poetry, merely because it is not invented, but the true utterance of a real person.

affecting result.   For instance, no one but a true
poet would have thought of exciting our pity for
a bereaved father by describing his way of lock-
ing the door of his house:

> " Perhaps to himself, at that moment he said,
>   The key I must take, for my Ellen is dead;
>   But of this in my ears not a word did he speak,
>   And he went to the chase with a tear on his cheek."

In like manner, in painting, it is altogether
impossible to say beforehand what details a
great painter may make poetical by his use of
them to excite noble emotions: and we shall,
therefore, find presently that a painting is to be
classed in the great or inferior schools, not according to the kind of details which it represents, but according to the uses for which it
employs them.

It is only farther to be noticed, that infinite
confusion has been introduced into this subject
by the careless and illogical custom of opposing
painting to poetry, instead of regarding poetry
as consisting in a noble use, whether of colors
or words.   Painting is properly to be opposed to
speaking or *writing*, but not to *poetry*. Both
painting and speaking are methods of expression.
Poetry is the employment of either for the
noblest purposes.

The imagination has three totally distinct
functions.   It combines, and by combination

creates new forms; but the secret principle of this combination has not been shown by the analysts. Again, it treats, or regards, both the simple images and its own combinations in peculiar ways; and thirdly, it penetrates, analyzes, and reaches truths by no other faculty discoverable.

The essential characters of composition, properly so called, are these. The mind which desires the new feature summons up before it those images which it supposes to be of the kind wanted, of these it takes the one which it supposes to be fittest, and tries it: if it will not answer, it tries another, until it has obtained such an association as pleases it.

In this operation, if it be of little sensibility, it regards only the absolute beauty or value of the images brought before it; and takes that or those which it thinks fairest or most interesting, without any regard to their sympathy with those for whose company they are destined.

In composition the mind can only take cognizance of likeness or dissimilarity, or of abstract beauty among the ideas it brings together. But neither likeness nor dissimilarity secures harmony. We saw in the chapter on unity that likeness destroyed harmony or unity of membership, and that difference did not necessarily secure it, but only that particular imperfection in each of the harmonizing parts which can only be supplied by its fellow part. If, therefore, the combination made is to be harmonious, the artist must induce in each of its component parts (suppose two only, for simplicity's sake,) such imperfection as that the other shall put it right. If one of them be perfect by itself, the other will be an excrescence. Both must be faulty when separate, and each corrected by the presence of the other. If he can accomplish this, the result will be beautiful; it will be a whole, an organized body with dependent members;—he is an inventor. If not, let his separate features be as beautiful, as opposite, or as resemblant as they may, they form no whole. They are two members glued together.

A powerfully imaginative mind seizes and combines at the same instant, not only two, but all the important ideas of its poem or picture, and while it works with any one of them, it is at the same instant working with and modifying all in their relations to it, never losing sight of their bearings on each other ; as the motion of a snake's body goes through all parts at once, and its volition acts at the same instant in coils that go contrary ways.

This faculty is indeed something that looks as if man were made after the image of God. It is inconceivable, admirable, altogether divine.

There is, however, a limit to the power of all human imagination. When the relations to be observed are absolutely necessary, and highly complicated, the mind cannot grasp them, and the result is a total deprivation of all power of imagination associative in such matter. For this reason, no human mind has ever conceived a new animal.

We have thus far been defining that combining operation of the imagination which appears to be in a sort mechanical; we must now examine its dealings with its separate conceptions.

Its function and gift are the getting at the root, its nature and dignity depend on its holding things always by the heart. Take its hand from off the beating of that, and it will prophesy no longer ; it looks not in the eyes, it judges not by the voice, it describes not by outward features, all that it affirms, judges, or describes, it affirms from within.

It drinks the very vital sap of that it deals with: once there it is at liberty to throw up what new shoots it will, so always that the true juice and sap be in them, and to prune and twist them at its pleasure, and bring them to fairer fruit than grew on the old tree.

It may seem to the reader that I am incorrect in calling this penetrating, possession-taking faculty, imagination. Be it so, the name is of

little consequence ; the faculty itself, called by
what name we will, I insist upon as the highest
intellectual power of man.   There is no reasoning in it, it works not by algebra, nor by integral
calculus, it is a piercing, Pholas-like mind's
tongue that works and tastes into the very rock
heart, no matter what be the subject submitted to
it, substance or spirit, all is alike, divided asunder, joint and marrow, whatever utmost truth,
life, principle, it has, laid bare, and that which
has no truth, life, nor principle, dissipated into
its original smoke at a touch.   The whispers at
men's ears it lifts into visible angels.   Vials that
have lain sealed in the deep sea a thousand years
it unseals, and brings out of them Genii.

Every great conception of poet or painter is
held and treated by this faculty.   Every character that is so much as touched by men like
Æschylus, Homer, Dante, or Shakspeare, is by
them held by the heart ; and every circumstance
or sentence of their being, speaking, or seeming, is
seized by process from within, and is referred to
that inner secret spring of which the hold is never
lost for an instant , so that every sentence, as it
has been thought out from the heart, opens for
us a way down to the heart, leads us to the
centre, and then leaves us to gather what more we
may ; it is the open sesame of a huge, obscure,
endless cave, with inexhaustible treasure of pure

gold scattered in it; the wandering about and gathering the pieces may be left to any of us, all can accomplish that; but the first opening of that invisible door in the rock is of the imagination only.

I believe it will be found that the entirely unimaginative mind *sees* nothing of the object it has to dwell upon or describe, and is therefore utterly unable, as it is blind itself, to set anything before the eyes of the reader.

The fancy sees the outside, and is able to give a portrait of the outside, clear, brilliant, and full of detail.

The imagination sees the heart and inner nature, and makes them felt, but is often obscure, mysterious, and interrupted, in its giving of outer detail.

Take an instance. A writer with neither imagination nor fancy, describing a fair lip, does not see it, but thinks about it, and about what is said of it, and calls it well-turned, or rosy, or delicate, or lovely, or afflicts us with some other quenching and chilling epithet. Now bear fancy speak,—

> " Her lips were red, and one was thin,
> Compared with that was next her chin,
> Some bee had stung it newly."

The real, red, bright being of the lip is there in a moment. But it is all outside; no expres-

sion yet, no mind.   Let us go a step farther with
Warner, of fair Rosamond struck by Eleanor.

> " With that she dashed her on the lips
>   So dyed double red;
>   Hard was the heart that gave the blow,
>   Soft were those lips that bled."

The tenderness of mind begins to mingle with
the outside color, the imagination is seen in its
awakening.   Next Shelley,—

> " Lamp of life, thy lips are burning
>   Through the veil that seems to hide them,
>   As the radiant lines of morning
>   Through thin clouds, ere they divide them."

In Milton it happens, I think, generally, and
in the case before us most certainly, that the
imagination is mixed and broken with fancy,
and so the strength of the imagery is part of iron
and part of clay.

" Bring the rathe primrose, that forsaken dies, (Imagi-
    nation)
The tufted crow-toe, and pale jessamine, (Nugatory)
The white pink, and the pansy freaked with jet, (Fancy)
The glowing violet, (Imagination)
The musk rose, and the well-attired woodbine, (Fancy,
    vulgar)
With cowslips wan, that hang the pensive head, (Imagina-
    tion)
And every flower that sad embroidery wears." (Mixed)

Fancy, as she stays at the externals, can
never feel.   She is one of the hardest hearted of

the intellectual faculties, or rather one of the most purely and simply intellectual. She cannot be made serious, no edge tools but she will play with; whereas the imagination is in all things the reverse. She cannot be but serious; she sees too far, too darkly, too solemnly, too earnestly, ever to smile. There is something in the heart of everything, if we can reach it, that we shall not be inclined to laugh at. The ανήριθμον γέλασμα of the sea is on its surface, not in the deep.

Now, observe, while, as it penetrates into the nature of things, the imagination is pre-eminently a beholder of things *as* they *are*, it is, in its creative function, an eminent beholder of things *when* and *where* they are NOT; a seer, that is, in the prophetic sense, calling " the things that are not as though they were," and for ever delighting to dwell on that which is not tangibly present. And its great function being the calling forth, or back, that which is not visible to bodily sense, it has of course been made to take delight in the fulfilment of its proper function, and pre-eminently to enjoy, and spend its energy, on things past and future, or out of sight, rather than things present, or in sight. So that if the imagination is to be called to take delight in any object, it will not be always well, if we can help it, to put the *real* object there, before it. The imagination would on the whole rather have it *not* there ;—the reality and substance are rather in the imagination's way ; it would think a good deal more of the thing if it could not see it. Hence, that strange and sometimes fatal charm, which is in all things as long as we wait for them, and the moment we have lost them ; but which fades while we possess them ;—that sweet bloom of all that is far away, which perishes under our touch.   Yet the feeling of this is not a weakness; it is one of the most glorious gifts of the human mind, making the whole infinite future, and imperishable past, a richer inheritance, if faithfully inherited, than the changeful, frail, fleeting present ; it is also one of the many witnesses in us to the truth that these present and tangible things are not meant to satisfy us. The instinct becomes a weakness only when it is weakly indulged, and when the faculty which was intended by God to give back to us what we have lost, and gild for us what is to come, is so perverted as only to darken what we possess. But, perverted or pure, the instinct itself is everlasting, and the substantial presence even of the things which we love the best, will inevitably and for ever be found wanting in *one* strange and tender charm, which belonged to the dreams of them.

Greatness in art (as assuredly in all other

things, but more distinctly in this than in most of them,) is not a teachable nor gainable thing, but *the expression of the mind of a God-made great man;* that teach, or preach, or labor as you will, everlasting difference is set between one man's capacity and another's; and that this God-given supremacy is the priceless thing, always just as rare in the world at one time as another. What you can manufacture, or communicate, you can lower the price of, but this mental supremacy is incommunicable; you will never multiply its quantity, nor lower its price; and nearly the best thing that men can generally do is to set themselves, not to the attainment, but the discovery of this; learning to know gold, when we see it, from iron-glance, and diamonds from flint-sand, being for most of us a more profitable employment than trying to make diamonds out of our own charcoal. And for this God-made supremacy, I generally have used, and shall continue to use, the word Inspiration, not carelessly nor lightly, but in all logical calmness and perfect reverence.

There is reciprocal action between the intensity of moral feeling and the power of imagination; for, on the one hand, those who have keenest sympathy are those who look closest, and pierce deepest, and hold securest; and, on the other, those who have so pierced and seen the melan-

choly deeps of things, are filled with the most
intense passion and gentleness of sympathy.
Hence, I suppose that the powers of the imagination may always be tested by accompanying
tenderness of emotion, and thus (as Byron said),
there is no tenderness like Dante's, neither any
intensity nor seriousness like his, such seriousness that it is incapable of perceiving that which
is commonplace or ridiculous, but fuses all down
into its white-hot fire. All egotism, and selfish
care, or regard, are in proportion to their constancy, destructive of imagination; whose play
and power depend altogether on our being able
to forget ourselves and enter like possessing
spirits into the bodies of things about us.

Again, as the life of imagination is in the discovering of truth, it is clear it can have no respect for sayings or opinions: knowing in itself
when it has invented truly—restless and tormented except when it has this knowledge, its
sense of success or failure is too acute to be affected by praise or blame. Sympathy it desires
—but can do without; of opinions it is regardless, not in pride, but because it has no vanity,
and is conscious of a rule of action and object
of aim in which it cannot be mistaken; partly,
also, in pure energy of desire and longing to do
and to invent more and more, which suffer it
not to suck the sweetness of praise—unless a

little, with the end of the rod in its hand, and without pausing in its march. It goes straight forward up the hill; no voices nor mutterings can turn it back, nor petrify it from its purpose.

The imagination must be fed constantly by external nature—after the illustrations we have given, this may seem mere truism, for it is clear that to the exercise of the penetrative faculty a subject of penetration is necessary; but I note it because many painters of powerful mind have been lost to the world by their suffering the restless writhing of their imagination in its cage to take place of its healthy and exulting activity in the fields of nature. The most imaginative men always study the hardest, and are the most thirsty for new knowledge. Fancy plays like a squirrel in its circular prison, and is happy; but imagination is a pilgrim on the earth—and her home is in heaven. Shut her from the fields of the celestial mountains—bar her from breathing their lofty, sun-warmed air; and we may as well turn upon her the last bolt of the tower of famine, and give the keys to the keeping of the wildest surge that washes Capraja and Gorgona.

Witness the operation of the imagination in Coleridge, on one of the most trifling objects that could possibly have been submitted to its action.

> " The thin blue flame
> Lies on my low burnt fire, and quivers not:
> Only that film which fluttered on the grate
> Still flutters there, the sole unquiet thing.
> Methinks its motion in this hush of nature
> Gives it dim sympathies with me, who live,
> Making it a companionable form,
> Whose puny flaps and freaks the idling spirit
> By its own moods interprets; everywhere
> Echo or mirror seeking of itself,
> And makes a toy of thought."

Observe the sweet operation of fancy, in the following well-known passage from Scott, where both her beholding and transforming powers are seen in their simplicity.

> " The rocky summits—split and rent,
> Formed turret, dome, or battlement.—
> Or seemed fantastically set
> With cupola or minaret.
> Nor were these earth-born castles bare,
> Nor lacked they many a banner fair,
> For from their shivered brows displayed,
> Far o'er th' unfathomable glade,
> All twinkling with the dew-drop sheen,
> The brier-rose fell, in streamers green,—
> And creeping shrubs of thousand dyes
> Waved in the west wind's summer sighs."

Compare with it the real and high action of the imagination on the same matter in Words-worth's Yew trees (which I consider the most

vigorous and solemn bit of forest landscape ever
painted):—

> "Each particular trunk a growth
> Of intertwisted fibres serpentine,
> Up coiling and inveterately convolved,
> *Nor uninformed with Phantasy, and looks*
> *That threaten the profane.*"

THE SUPERNATURAL.

There are four ways in which beings supernatural may be conceived as manifesting themselves
to human sense. The first, by external types,
signs, or influences; as God to Moses in the
flames of the bush, and to Elijah in the voice of
Horeb.

The second, by the assuming of a form not
properly belonging to them; as the Holy Spirit
of that of a dove, the second person of the
Trinity of that of a Lamb; and so such manifestations, under angelic or other form, of the first
person of the Trinity, as seem to have been
made to Abraham, Moses, and Ezekiel.

The third, by the manifestation of a form
properly belonging to them, but not necessarily
seen; as of the Risen Christ to his disciples when
the doors were shut. And the fourth, by their
operation on the human form, which they influ-

ence or inspire, as in the shining of the face of Moses.

It is evident that in all these cases, wherever there is form at all, it is the form of some creature to us known. It is no new form peculiar to spirit, nor can it be. We can conceive of none. Our inquiry is simply, therefore, by what modifications those creature forms to us known, as of a lamb, a bird, or a human creature, may be explained as signs or habitations of Divinity, or of angelic essence, and not creatures such as they seem.

This may be done in two ways. First, by effecting some change in the appearance of the creature inconsistent with its actual nature, as by giving it colossal size, or unnatural color, or material, as of gold, or silver, or flame, instead of flesh, or by taking away its property of matter altogether, and forming it of light or shade, or in an intermediate step, of cloud, or vapor; or explaining it by terrible concomitant circumstances, as of wounds in the body, or strange lights and seemings round about it; or by joining of two bodies together as in angels' wings. Of all which means of attaining supernatural character (which, though in their nature ordinary and vulgar, are yet effective and very glorious in mighty hands) we have already seen the limits in speaking of the imagination.

But the second means of obtaining supernatural character is that with which we are now concerned, namely, retaining the actual form in its full and material presence, and without aid from any external interpretation whatever, to raise that form by mere inherent dignity to such a pitch of power and impressiveness as cannot but assert and stamp it for superhuman.

He who can do this has reached the last pinnacle and utmost power of ideal, or any other art. He stands in no need, thenceforward, of cloud, nor lightning, nor tempest, nor terror of mystery. His sublime is independent of the elements. It is of that which shall stand when they shall melt with fervent heat, and light the firmament when the sun is as sackcloth of hair.

The Greek could not conceive a spirit; he could do nothing without limbs; his god is a finite god, talking, pursuing, and going journeys; if at any time he was touched with a true feeling of the unseen powers around him, it was in the field of poised battle, for there is something in the near coming of the shadow of death, something in the devoted fulfilment of mortal duty, that reveals the real God, though darkly; that pause on the field of Platæa was not one of vain superstition; the two white figures that blazed along the Delphic plain, when the earthquake

and the fire led the charge from Olympus, were
more than sunbeams on the battle dust; the
sacred cloud, with its lance light and triumph
singing, that went down to brood over the masts of
Salamis, was more than morning mist among the
olives: and yet what were the Greek's thoughts
of his god of battle? No spirit power was in the
vision; it was a being of clay strength and human
passion, foul, fierce, and changeful; of penetra-
ble arms, and vulnerable flesh. Gather what we
may of great, from pagan chisel or pagan dream,
and set it beside the orderer of Christian warfare,
Michael the Archangel: not Milton's "with hos-
tile brow and visage all inflamed," not even
Milton's in kingly treading of the hills of Paradise, not Raffaelle's with the expanded wings
and brandished spear, but Perugino's with his
triple crest of traceless plume unshaken in
heaven, his hand fallen on his crossleted sword,
the truth girdle binding his undinted armor;
God has put his power upon him, resistless
radiance is on his limbs, no lines are there of
earthly strength, no trace on the divine features
of earthly anger; trustful and thoughtful, fear-
less, but full of love, incapable except of the
repose of eternal conquest, vessel and instrument of Omnipotence, filled like a cloud with
the victor light, the dust of principalities and
powers beneath his feet, the murmur of hell

against him heard by his spiritual ear like the winding of a shell on the far off sea-shore.

It is vain to attempt to pursue the comparison; the two orders of art have in them nothing common, and the field of sacred history, the intent and scope of Christian feeling, are too wide and exalted to admit of the juxtaposition of any other sphere or order of conception; they embrace all other fields like the dome of heaven. With what comparison shall we compare the types of the martyr saints, the St. Stephen of Fra Bartolomeo, with his calm forehead crowned by the stony diadem, or the St. Catherine of Raffaelle looking up to heaven in the dawn of the eternal day, with her lips parted in the resting from her pain? or with what the Madonnas of Francia and Pinturicchio, in whom the hues of the morning and the solemnity of eve, the gladness in accomplished promise, and sorrow of the sword-pierced heart, are gathered into one human lamp of ineffable love? or with what the angel choirs of Angelico, with the flames on their white foreheads waving brighter as they move, and the sparkles streaming from their purple wings like the glitter of many suns upon a sounding sea, listening, in the pauses of alternate song, for the prolonging of the trumpet blast, and the answering of psaltery and cymbal, throughout the endless deep and from all the star shores of heaven?

Bacon and Pascal appear to be men naturally very similar in their temper and powers of mind. One, born in York House, Strand, of courtly parents, educated in court atmosphere, and re-plying, almost as soon as he could speak, to the queen asking how old he was—"Two years younger than Your Majesty's happy reign!"—has the world's meanness and cunning engrafted into his intellect, and remains smooth, serene, unenthusiastic, and in some degree base, even with all his sincere devotion and universal wisdom; bearing, to the end of life, the likeness of a marble palace in the street of a great city, fairly furnished within, and bright in wall and battlement, yet noisome in places about the foundations.   The other, born at Cleremont, in Auvergne, under the shadow of the Puy de Dôme, though taken to Paris at eight years old, retains for ever the impress of his birthplace; pursuing natural philosophy with the same zeal as Bacon, he returns to his own mountains to put himself under their tutelage, and by their help first dis-covers the great relations of the earth and the air: struck at last with mortal disease; gloomy, enthusiastic, and superstitious, with a conscience burning like lava, and inflexible like iron, the clouds gather about the majesty of him, fold after fold; and, with his spirit buried in ashes, and rent by earthquake, yet fruitful of true thought and faithful affection, he stands like that mound of desolate scoria that crowns the hill ranges of his native land, with its sable summit far in heaven, and its foundations green with the ordered garden and the trellised vine.

When, however, our inquiry thus branches into the successive analysis of individual characters, it is time for us to leave it; noting only one or two points respecting Shakspeare. He seems to have been sent essentially to take universal and equal grasp of the *human* nature; and to have been removed, therefore, from all influences which could in the least warp or bias his thoughts. It was necessary that he should lean *no* way; that he should contemplate, with absolute equality of judgment, the life of the court, cloister, and tavern, and be able to sympathize so completely with all creatures as to deprive himself, together with his personal identity, even of his conscience, as he casts himself into their hearts. He must be able to enter into the soul of Falstaff or Shylock with no more sense of contempt or horror than Falstaff or Shylock themselves feel for or in themselves; otherwise his own conscience and indignation would make him unjust to them; he would turn aside from

something, miss some good, or overlook some
essential palliation. He must be utterly without
anger, utterly without purpose; for if a man has
any serious purpose in life, that which runs
counter to it, or is foreign to it, will be looked
at frowningly or carelessly by him. Shakspeare
was forbidden of Heaven to have any *plans*. To
do any good or *get* any good, in the common
sense of good, was not to be within his permitted
range of work. Not, for him, the founding of
institutions, the preaching of doctrines, or the
repression of abuses. Neither he, nor the sun,
did, on any morning that they rose together, receive charge from their Maker concerning such
things. They were both of them to shine on the
evil and good; both to behold unoffendedly all
that was upon the earth, to burn unappalled
upon the spears of kings, and undisdaining, upon
the reeds of the river.

Therefore, so far as nature had influence over
the early training of this man, it was essential to
his perfectness that the nature should be quiet.
No mountain passions were to be allowed in him.
Inflict upon him but one pang of the monastic
conscience; cast upon him but one cloud of the
mountain gloom; and his serenity had been gone
for ever—his equity—his infinity. You would
have made another Dante of him; and all that
he would have ever uttered about poor, soiled,

and frail humanity would have been the quarrel
between Sinon and Adam of Brescia,—speedily
retired from, as not worthy a man's hearing, nay
not to be heard without heavy fault. All your
Falstaffs, Slenders, Quicklys, Sir Tobys, Lances,
Touchstones, and Quinces would have been lost
in that. Shakspeare could be allowed no mountains; nay, not even any supreme natural beauty.
He had to be left with his kingcups and clover;
—pansies—the passing clouds—the Avon's flow
—and the undulating hills and woods of War-
wick; nay, he was not to love even these in any
exceeding measure, lest it might make him in
the least overrate their power upon the strong,
full-fledged minds of men. He makes the quar-
relling fairies concerned about them; poor lost
Ophelia find some comfort in them; fearful, fair,
wise-hearted Perdita trust the speaking of her
good will and good hostess-ship to them; and
one of the brothers of Imogen confide his sorrow to them,—rebuked instantly by his brother
for "wench-like words;"* but any thought of

---

* "With fairest flowers
While summer lasts, and I live here, Fidele,
I'll sweeten thy sad grave.   Thou shalt not lack
The flower that's like thy face—pale primrose, nor
The azured harebell—like thy veins ; no, nor
The leaf of eglantine, whom not to slander,
Outsweetened not thy breath.   The ruddock would

them in his mighty men I do not find: it is not
usually in the nature of such men; and if he had
loved the flowers the *least* better himself, he
would assuredly have been offended at this, and
given a botanical turn of mind to Cæsar or
Othello.

And it is even among the most curious proofs
of the necessity to all high imagination that it
should paint straight from the life, that he has
not given such a turn of mind to some of his great
men;—Henry the Fifth, for instance. Doubtless some of my readers, having been accustomed
to hear it repeated thoughtlessly from mouth
to mouth that Shakspeare conceived the spirit
of all ages, were as much offended as surprised

With charitable bill bring thee all this;
Yea, and furred moss besides, when flowers are none,
To winter-ground thy corse.

 Gui.   Prithee, have done,
 And do not play in wench-like words with that
 Which is so serious."

Imogen herself, afterwards in deeper passion, will give
weeds—not flowers—and something more:

         " And when
 With wildwood leaves, and weeds, I have
  strewed his grave,
 And on it said a century of prayers,
 Such as I can, twice o'er, I'll weep and sigh,
 And, leaving so his service, follow you."

at my saying that he only painted human nature as he saw it in his own time. They will find, if they look into his work closely, as much antiquarianism as they do geography, and no more. The commonly received notions about the things that had been, Shakspeare took as he found them, animating them with pure human nature, of any time and all time; but inquiries into the minor detail of temporary feeling, he despised as utterly as he did maps; and wheresoever the temporary feeling was in anywise contrary to that of his own day, he errs frankly, and paints from his own time. For instance in this matter of love of flowers; we have traced already, far enough for our general purposes, the mediæval interest in them, whether to be enjoyed in the fields, or to be used for types of ornamentation in dress. If Shakspeare had cared to enter into the spirit even of the early fifteenth century, he would assuredly have marked this affection in some of his knights, and indicated, even then, in heroic tempers, the peculiar respect for loveliness of *dress* which we find constantly in Dante. But he could not do this; he had not seen it in real life. In his time dress had become an affectation and absurdity. Only fools, or wise men in their weak moments, showed much concern about it; and the facts of human nature which appeared to him general in the matter

were the soldier's disdain, and the coxcomb's
care of it.   Hence Shakspeare's good soldier is
almost always in plain or battered armor; even
the speech of Vernon in Henry the Fourth,
which, as far as I remember, is the only one that
bears fully upon the beauty of armor, leans more
upon the spirit and hearts of men—" bated, like
eagles having lately bathed;" and has an undercurrent of slight contempt running through the
following line, " Glittering in golden coats, *like
images;*" while the beauty of the young Harry is
essentially the beauty of fiery and perfect youth,
answering as much to the Greek, or Roman, or
Elizabethan knight as to the mediæval one;
whereas the definite interest in armor and dress
is opposed by Shakspeare in the French (meaning to depreciate them), to the English rude sol-
dierliness:

" *Con*.   Tut, I have the best armor of the World.
Would it were day.
Ori.   You have an excellent armor, but let my horse
have his due."

  And again:

" My lord constable, the armor that I saw in your tent
to-night, are those stars, or suns, upon it ?"

while Henry, half proud of his poorness of ar-
ray, speaks of armorial splendor scornfully ; the

main idea being still of its being a gilded show and vanity—

" Our gayness and our *gilt* are all besmirched."

This is essentially Elizabethan. The quarterings on a knight's shield, or the inlaying of his armor, would never have been thought of by him as mere " gayness or gilt" in earlier days.* In like manner, throughout every scale of rank or feeling, from that of the French knights down to Falstaff's " I looked he should have sent me two-and-twenty yards of satin, as I am true knight, and he sends me security !" care for dress is always considered by Shakspeare as contemptible; and Mrs. Quickly distinguishes herself from a true fairy by her solicitude to scour the *chairs of order*—and " each fair instalment, coat, and several crest ;" and the association in her mind of the flowers in the fairy rings with the

" Sapphire, pearl, and rich embroidery,
    Buckled below fair knighthood's bending knee;"

while the true fairies, in field simplicity, are only anxious to ' sweep the dust behind the door;' and

---

* If the reader thinks that in Henry the Fifth's time the Elizabethan temper might already have been manifesting itself, let him compare the English herald's speech, act 2, scene 2, of King John ; and by way of specimen of Shakspeare's historical care, or regard of mediæval character, the large use of *artillery* in the previous scene.

> " With this field dew consecrate,
> Every several chamber bless
> Through this palace with sweet peace."

Note the expression " Field dew consecrate."
Shakspeare loved courts and camps ; but he felt
that sacredness and peace were in the dew of the
Fields only.

There is another respect in which he was
wholly incapable of entering into the spirit of
the middle ages. He had no great art of any
kind around him in his own country, and was,
consequently, just as powerless to conceive the
general influence of former art, as a man of the
most inferior calibre. Therefore it was, that I
did not care to quote his authority when speaking on a former occasion respecting the power of
imitation. If it had been needful to add his
testimony to that of Dante, I might have quoted
multitudes of passages wholly concurring with
that, of which the " fair Portia's counterfeit,"
with the following lines, and the implied ideal of
sculpture in the Winter's Tale, are wholly unanswerable instances. But Shakspeare's evidence
in matters of art is as narrow as the range of
Elizabethan art in England, and resolves itself
wholly into admiration of two things,—mockery
of life (as in this instance of Hermione as a
statue), or absolute splendor, as in the close of
Romeo and Juliet, where the notion of *gold* as

the chief source of dignity of aspect, coming down to Shakspeare from the times of the Field of the Cloth of Gold, and, as I said before, strictly Elizabethan, would interfere seriously with the pathos of the whole passage, but for the sense of sacrifice implied in it :

> " As *rich* shall Romeo by his lady lie,
> Poor sacrifices of our enmity."

And observe, I am not giving these examples as proof of any smallness in Shakspeare, but of his greatness ; that is to say, of his contentment, like every other great man who ever breathed, to paint nothing but *what he saw ;* and therefore giving perpetual evidence that his sight was of the sixteenth, and not of the thirteenth century, beneath all the broad and eternal humanity of his imagination. How far in these modern days, emptied of splendor, it may be necessary to great men having certain sympathies for those earlier ages, to act in this differently from all their predecessors ; and how far they may succeed in the resuscitation of the past by habitually dwelling in all their thoughts among vanished generations, are questions, of all practical and present ones concerning art, the most difficult to decide ; for already in poetry several of our truest men have set themselves to this task, and have indeed put more vitality into the shadows

of the dead than most others can give the presences of the living. Thus Longfellow, in the
Golden Legend, has entered more closely into
the temper of the Monk, for good and for evil,
than ever yet theological writer or historian,
though they may have given their life's labor to
the analysis : and, again, Robert Browning is
unerring in every sentence he writes of the middle ages.

At the close of the last century, the architecture, domestic life and manners were gradually getting more and more artificial ; all natural
beauty had ceased to be permitted in architectural decoration, while the habits of society led
them more and more to live, if possible, in cities;
and the dress, language, and manners of men, in
general, were approximating to that horrible and
lifeless condition in which you find them, just
before the outbreak of the French Revolution.

Now, observe : exactly as hoops, and starch,
and false hair, and all that in mind and heart
these things typify and betray, as these, I say,
gained upon men, there was a necessary reaction
in favor of the *natural.* Men had never lived so
utterly in defiance of the laws of nature before ;
but they could not do this without feeling a
strange charm in that which they defied ; and
accordingly we find this reactionary sentiment

expressing itself in a base school of what was called *pastoral* poetry; that is to say, poetry written in praise of the country, by men who lived in coffee-houses and on the Mall. The essence of pastoral poetry is the sense of strange delightfulness in grass, which is occasionally felt by a man who has seldom set his foot on it; it is essentially the poetry of the cockney, and for the most part corresponds in its aim and rank, as compared with other literature, to the porcelain shepherds and shepherdesses on a chimneypiece as compared with great works of sculpture.

Of course all good poetry, descriptive of rural life, is essentially pastoral, or has the effect of the pastoral, on the minds of men living in cities; but the class of poetry which I mean, and which you probably understand, by the term pastoral, is that in which a farmer's girl is spoken of as a "nymph," and a farmer's boy as a "swain," and in which, throughout, a ridiculous and unnatural refinement is supposed to exist in rural life, merely because the poet himself has neither had the courage to endure its hardships, nor the wit to conceive its realities. If you examine the literature of the past century, you will find that nearly all its expressions, having reference to the country, show something of this kind; either a foolish sentimentality, or a morbid fear, both of course coupled with the most curious ignorance.

You will find all its descriptive expressions at once vague and monotonous. Brooks are always " purling ;" birds always "warbling ;" mountains always "lift their horrid peaks above the clouds;" vales always " are lost in the shadow of gloomy woods ;" a few more distinct ideas about hay-making and curds and cream, acquired in the neighborhood of Richmond Bridge, serving to give an occasional appearance of freshness to the catalogue of the sublime and beautiful which descended from poet to poet ; while a few true pieces of pastoral, like the " Vicar of Wakefield," and Walton's " Angler," relieved the general waste of dulness. Even in these better productions, nothing is more remarkable than the general conception of the country merely as a series of green fields, and the combined ignorance and dread of more sublime scenery; of which the mysteries and dangers were enhanced by the difficulties of travelling at the period. Thus in Walton's " Angler," you have a meeting of two friends, one a Derbyshireman, the other a lowland traveller, who is as much alarmed, and uses nearly as many expressions of astonishment, at having to go down a steep hill and ford a brook, as a traveller uses now at crossing the glacier of the Col de Geant. I am not sure whether the difficulties which, until late years, have lain in the way of peaceful and convenient travelling, ought not to have great weight assigned to them among the other causes of the temper of the century; but be that as it may, if you will examine the whole range of its literature—keeping this point in view—I am well persuaded that you will be struck most forcibly by the strange deadness to the higher sources of landscape sublimity which is mingled with the morbid pastoralism. The love of fresh air and green grass forced itself upon the animal natures of men; but that of the sublimer features of scenery had no place in minds whose chief powers had been repressed by the formalisms of the age. And although in the second-rate writers continually, and in the first-rate ones occasionally, you find an affectation of interest in mountains, clouds, and forests, yet whenever they write from their heart, you will find an utter absence of feeling respecting anything beyond gardens and grass. Examine, for instance, the novels of Smollett, Fielding, and Sterne, the comedies of Molière, and the writings of Johnson and Addison, and I do not think you will find a single expression of true delight in sublime nature in any one of them. Perhaps Sterne's "Sentimental Journey," in its total absence of sentiment on any subject but humanity, and its entire want of notice of anything at Geneva, which might not as well have been seen at Coxwold, is the most

striking instance I could give you; and if you
compare with this negation of feeling on one
side, the interludes of Molière, in which shepherds and shepherdesses are introduced in court
dress, you have a very accurate conception of
the general spirit of the age.

It was in such a state of society that the
landscape of Claude, Gaspar Poussin, and Salvator Rosa attained its reputation.   It is the complete expression on canvas of the spirit of the
time.   Claude embodies the foolish pastoralism,
Salvator the ignorant terror, and Gaspar the dull
and affected erudition.

It was, however, altogether impossible that
this state of things could long continue. The age
which had buried itself in formalism grew weary
at last of the restraint; and the approach of a
new æra was marked by the appearance, and
the enthusiastic reception, of writers who took
delight in those wild scenes of nature which had
so long been despised.

I think the first two writers in whom the symptoms of a change are strongly manifested are
Mrs. Radcliffe and Rousseau; in both of whom
the love of natural scenery, though mingled in
the one case with what was merely dramatic,
and in the other with much that was pitifully
morbid or vicious, was still itself genuine, and
intense, differing altogether in character from

any sentiments previously traceable in literature. And then rapidly followed a group of writers, who expressed, in various ways, the more powerful or more pure feeling which had now become one of the strongest instincts of the age. Of these, the principal is Walter Scott. Many writers, indeed, describe nature more minutely and more profoundly; but none show in higher intensity the peculiar passion for what is majestic or lovely in *wild* nature, to which I am now referring. The whole of the poem of the " Lady of the Lake " is written with almost a boyish enthusiasm for rocks, and lakes, and cataracts; the early novels show the same instinct in equal strength wherever he approaches Highland scenery; and the feeling is mingled, observe, with a most touching and affectionate appreciation of the Gothic architecture, in which alone he found the elements of natural beauty seized by art; so that, to this day, his descriptions of Melrose and Holy Island Cathedral, in the " Lay of the Last Minstrel " and " Marmion," as well as of the ideal abbeys in the " Monastery " and " Antiquary," together with those of Caerlaverock and Lochleven Castles in "Guy Mannering " and "The Abbot," remain the staple possessions and text-books of all travellers, not so much for their beauty or accuracy, as for their *exactly expressing that degree of*

*feeling with which most men in this century can
sympathize.*

Together with Scott appeared the group of
poets,—Byron, Wordsworth, Keats, Shelley, and,
finally, Tennyson,—differing widely in moral
principles and spiritual temper, but all agreeing
more or less in this love for natural scenery.

Now, you will ask me—and you will ask me
most reasonably—how this love of nature in
modern days can be connected with Christianity, seeing it is as strong in the infidel Shelley as
in the sacred Wordsworth. Yes, and it was
found in far worse men than Shelley. Shelley
was an honest unbeliever, and a man of warm
affections; but this new love of nature is found
in the most reckless and unprincipled of the
French novelists,—in Eugene Sue, in Dumas, in
George Sand,—and that intensely. How is
this? Simply because the feeling is reactionary;
and, in this phase of it, common to the diseased
mind as well as to the healthy one. A man dy-
ing in the fever of intemperance will cry out for
water, and that with a bitterer thirst than a man
whose healthy frame naturally delights in the
mountain spring more than in the wine cup.
The water is not dishonored by the thirst of that
diseased, nor is nature dishonored by the love
of the unworthy. That love is, perhaps, the
only saving element in their minds; and it still

remains an indisputable truth that the love of
nature is a characteristic of the Christian heart,
just as the hunger for healthy food is characteristic of the healthy frame.

I think it probable that many readers may be
surprised at my calling Scott the great representative of the mind of the age in literature.
Those who can perceive the intense penetrative
depth of Wordsworth, and the exquisite finish
and melodious power of Tennyson, may be offended at my placing in higher rank that poetry
of careless glance, and reckless rhyme, in which
Scott poured out the fancies of his youth; and
those who are familiar with the subtle analysis
of the French novelists, or who have in any wise
submitted themselves to the influence of German philosophy, may be equally indignant at
my ascribing a principality to Scott among the
literary men of Europe, in an age which has
produced De Balzac and Goethe.

I believe the first test of a truly great man is
his humility. I do not mean, by humility, doubt
of his own power, or hesitation in speaking of
his opinions; but a right understanding of the
relation between what *he* can do and say, and
the rest of the world's sayings and doings. All
great men not only know their business, but usually know that they know it; and are not only

right in their main opinions, but they usually
know that they are right in them; only they do
not think much of themselves on that account.
Arnolfo knows he can build a good dome at
Florence; Albert Durer writes calmly to one
who had found fault with his work, " It cannot
be better done;" Sir Isaac Newton knows that
he has worked out a problem or two that would
have puzzled anybody else;—only they do not
expect their fellow-men therefore to fall down
and worship them; they have a curious under-
sense of powerlessness, feeling that the greatness
is not *in* them, but *through* them; that they
could not do or be anything else than God made
them.   And they see something divine and God-
made in every other man they meet, and are
endlessly, foolishly, and incredibly merciful.

Now, I find among the men of the present
age, as far as I know them, this character in
Scott and Turner pre-eminently; I am not sure
if it is not in them alone.   I do not find Scott
talking about the dignity of literature, nor Turner about the dignity of painting.   They do
their work, feeling that they cannot well help it;
the story must be told, and the effect put down ;
and if people like it, well and good; and if not,
the world will not be much the worse.

I believe a very different impression of their
estimate of themselves and their doings will be

received by any one who reads the conversation of Wordsworth or Goethe. The *slightest* manifestation of jealousy or self-complacency is enough to mark a second-rate character of the intellect; and I fear that, especially in Goethe, such manifestations are neither few nor slight.

Connected with this general humility is the total absence of affectation in these men,—that is to say, of any assumption of manner or behavior in their work, in order to attract attention. Not but that they are mannerists both. Scott's verse is strongly mannered, and Turner's oil painting; but the manner of it is necessitated by the feelings of the men, entirely natural to both, never exaggerated for the sake of show. I hardly know any other literary or pictorial work of the day which is not in some degree affected. I am afraid Wordsworth was often affected in his simplicity, and De Balzac in his finish. Many fine French writers are affected in their reserve, and full of stage tricks in placing of sentences. It is lucky if in German writers we ever find so much as a sentence without affectation.

Again: another very important, though not infallible test of greatness is, as we have often said, the appearance of Ease with which the thing is done. It may be that, as with Dante and Leonardo, the finish given to the work effaces the evidence of ease; but where the ease is manifest, as in Scott, Turner, and Tintoret, and the thing done is very noble, it is a strong reason for placing the men above those who confessedly work with great pains. Scott writing his chapter or two before breakfast—not retouching, Turner finishing a whole drawing in a forenoon before he goes to shoot (providing always the chapter and drawing be good), are instantly to be set above men who confessedly have spent the day over the work, and think the hours well spent if it has been a little mended between sunrise and sunset. Indeed, it is no use for men to think to appear great by working fast, dashing, and scrawling; the thing they do must be good and great, cost what time it may; but if it *be* so, and they have honestly and unaffectedly done it with *no effort*, it is probably a greater and better thing than the result of the hardest efforts of others.

Then, as touching the kind of work done by these two men, the more I think of it I find this conclusion more impressed upon me,—that the greatest thing a human soul ever does in this world is to *see* something, and tell what it *saw* in a plain way. Hundreds of people can talk for one who can think, but thousands can think for one who can see. To see clearly, is poetry, prophecy, and religion,—all in one.

Therefore, finding the world of Literature more or less divided into Thinkers and Seers, I believe we shall find also that the Seers are wholly the greater race of the two. A true Thinker who has practical purpose in his thinking, and is sincere, as Plato, or Carlyle, or Helps, becomes in some sort a seer, and must be always of infinite use in his generation ; but an affected Thinker, who supposes his thinking of any other importance than as it tends to work, is about the vainest kind of person that can be found in the occupied classes. Nay, I believe that metaphysicians and philosophers are, on the whole, the greatest troubles the world has got to deal with; and that while a tyrant or bad man is of some use in teaching people submission or indignation, and a thoroughly idle man is only harmful in setting an idle example, and communicating to other lazy people his own lazy misunderstandings, busy metaphysicians are always entangling *good* and *active* people, and weaving cobwebs among the finest wheels of the world's business ; and are as much as possible, by all prudent persons, to be brushed out of their way, like spiders, and the meshed weed that has got into the Cambridgeshire canals, and other such impediments to barges and business. And if we thus clear the metaphysical element out of modern literature. we shall find its bulk amazingly diminished, and the claims of the remaining writers, or of those whom we have thinned by this abstraction of their straw stuffing, much more easily adjusted.*

Again: the mass of sentimental literature, concerned with the analysis and description of emotion, headed by the poetry of Byron, is altogether of lower rank than the literature which merely describes what it saw. The true Seer always feels as intensely as any one else; but he does not much describe his feelings. He tells you whom he met, and what they said, leaves you to make out, from that, what they feel, and what he feels, but goes into little detail. And, generally speaking, pathetic writing and careful explanation of passion are quite easy, compared with this plain recording of what people said or did, or with the right invention of what they are likely to say or do; for this reason, that to invent a story, or admirably and thoroughly tell any part of a story, it is necessary to grasp the

---

* Observe, I do not speak thus of metaphysics because I have no pleasure in them. When I speak contemptuously of philology, it may be answered me, that I am a bad scholar; but I cannot be so answered touching metaphysics, for every one conversant with such subjects may see that I have strong inclination that way, which would indeed, have led me far astray long ago, if I had not learned also some use of my hands, eyes, and feet.

entire mind of every personage concerned in it, and know precisely how they would be affected by what happens; which to do requires a colossal intellect; but to describe a separate emotion delicately, it is only needed that one should feel it oneself; and thousands of people are capable of feeling this or that noble emotion, for one who is able to enter into all the feelings of somebody sitting on the other side of the table. Even, therefore, when this sentimental literature is first rate, as in passages of Byron, Tennyson, and Keats, it ought not to be ranked so high as the Creative; and though perfection, even in narrow fields, is perhaps as rare as in the wider, and it may be as long before we have another In Memoriam as another Guy Mannering, I unhesitatingly receive as a greater manifestation of power the right invention of a few sentences spoken by Pleydell and Mannering across their supper-table, than the most tender and passionate melodies of the self-examining verse.

Having, therefore, cast metaphysical writers out of our way, and sentimental writers into the second rank, I do not think Scott's supremacy among those who remain will any more be doubtful; nor would it, perhaps, have been doubtful before, had it not been encumbered by innumerable faults and weaknesses. But it is

pre-eminently in these faults and weaknesses
that Scott is representative of the mind of his
age: and because he is the greatest man born
amongst us, and intended for the enduring type
of us, all our principal faults must be laid on his
shoulders, and he must bear down the dark
marks to the latest ages; while the smaller men,
who have some special work to do, perhaps not
so much belonging to this age as leading out of
it to the next, are often kept providentially quit
of the encumbrances which they had not
strength to sustain, and are much smoother and
pleasanter to look at, in their way; only that is
a smaller way.

Thus, the most startling fault of the age being
its faithlessness, it is necessary that its greatest
man should be faithless. Nothing is more notable or sorrowful in Scott's mind than its incapacity of steady belief in anything. He cannot
even resolve hardily to believe in a ghost, or a
water-spirit ; always explains them away in an
apologetic manner, not believing, all the while,
even his own explanation. He never can clearly
ascertain whether there is anything behind the
arras but rats ; never draws swords, and thrusts
at it for life or death ; but goes on looking at it
timidly, and saying, "it must be the wind." He
is educated a Presbyterian, and remains one,
because it is the most sensible thing he can do

if he is to live in Edinburgh ; but he thinks Romanism more picturesque, and profaneness more gentlemanly: does not see that anything affects human life but love, courage, and destiny ; which are, indeed, not matters of faith at all, but of sight. Any gods but those are very misty in outline to him ; and when the love is laid ghastly in poor Charlotte's coffin; and the courage is no more of use,—the pen having fallen from between the fingers ; and destiny is sealing the scroll,—the God-light is dim in the tears that fall on it.

He is in all this the epitome of his epoch.

Again: as another notable weakness of the age is its habit of looking back, in a romantic and passionate idleness, to the past ages, not understanding them all the while, nor really desiring to understand them, so Scott gives up nearly the half of his intellectual power to a fond, yet purposeless, dreaming over the past, and spends half his literary labors in endeavors to revive it, not in reality, but on the stage of fiction ; endeavors which were the best of the kind that modernism made, but still successful only so far as Scott put, under the old armor, the everlasting human nature which he knew ; and totally unsuccessful, so far as concerned the painting of the armor itself, which he knew *not*. The excellence of Scott's work is precisely in proportion

to the degree in which it is sketched from present nature. His familiar life is inimitable ; his
quiet scenes of introductory conversation, as the
beginning of Rob Roy and Redgauntlet, and all
his living Scotch characters, mean or noble,
from Andrew Fairservice to Jeanie Deans, are
simply right, and can never be bettered. But
his romance and antiquarianism, his knighthood
and monkery, are all false, and he knows them
to be false ; does not care to make them earnest ;
enjoys them for their strangeness, but laughs at
his own antiquarianism, all through his own third
novel,—with exquisite modesty indeed, but with
total misunderstanding of the function of an
Antiquary. He does not see how anything is to
be got out of the past but confusion, old iron on
drawing-room chairs, and serious inconvenience
to Dr. Heavysterne.

Again: more than any age that had preceded
it, ours had been ignorant of the meaning of the
word "Art." It had not a single fixed principle,
and what unfixed principles it worked upon were
all wrong. It was necessary that Scott should
know nothing of art. He neither cared for
painting nor sculpture, and was totally incapable
of forming a judgment about them. He had
some confused love of Gothic architecture, because it was dark, picturesque, old, and like
nature : but could not tell the worst from the

best, and built for himself perhaps the most in-
congruous and ugly pile that gentlemanly modernism ever designed ; marking, in the most curious
and subtle way, that mingling of reverence with
irreverence which is so striking in the age ; he
reverences Melrose, yet casts one of its piscinas,
puts a modern steel grate into it, and makes it his
fireplace. Like all pure moderns, he supposes
the Gothic barbarous, notwithstanding his love
of it ; admires, in an equally ignorant way,
totally opposite styles ; is delighted with the
new town of Edinburgh ; mistakes its dulness
for purity of taste, and actually compares it, in
its deathful formality of street, as contrasted
with the rudeness of the old town, to Britomart
taking off her armor.

Again: as in reverence and irreverence, so in
levity and melancholy, we saw that the spirit of
the age was strangely interwoven. Therefore,
also, it is necessary that Scott should be light,
careless, unearnest, and yet eminently sorrowful.
Throughout all his work there is no evidence of
any purpose but to while away the hour. His
life had no other object than the pleasure of the
instant, and the establishing of a family name.
All thoughts were, in their outcome and end, less
than nothing, and vanity. And yet, of all poetry
that I know, none is so sorrowful as Scott's.
Other great masters are pathetic in a resolute

and predetermined way, when they choose ; but, in their own minds, are evidently stern, or hopeful, or serene ; never really melancholy. Even Byron is rather sulky and desperate than melancholy ; Keats is sad because he is sickly ; Shelley because he is impious ; but Scott is inherently and consistently sad. Around all his power, and brightness, and enjoyment of eye and heart, the far-away Æolian knell is for ever sounding ; there is not one of those loving or laughing glances of his but it is brighter for the film of tears ; his mind is like one of his own hill rivers, —it is white, and flashes in the sun fairly, careless, as it seems, and hasty in its going, but

> " Far beneath, where slow they creep
> From pool to eddy, dark and deep,
> Where alders moist, and willows weep,
> You hear her streams repine."

Life begins to pass from him very early ; and while Homer sings cheerfully in his blindness, and Dante retains his courage, and rejoices in hope of Paradise, through all his exile, Scott, yet hardly past his youth, lies pensive in the sweet sunshine and among the harvest of his native hills.

> " Blackford, on whose uncultured breast,
> Among the broom, and thorn, and whin,
> A truant boy, I sought the nest,
> Or listed as I lay at rest,

> While rose on breezes thin
> The murmur of the city crowd,
> And, from his steeple jangling loud,
> St. Giles's mingling din!
> Now, from the summit to the plain,
> Waves all the hill with yellow grain,
>   And on the landscape as I look,
> Nought do I see unchanged remain,
>   Save the rude cliffs and chiming brook;
> To me they make a heavy moan
> Of early friendships past and gone.''

Such, then, being the weaknesses which it was necessary that Scott should share with his age, in order that he might sufficiently represent it, and such the grounds for supposing him, in spite of all these weaknesses, the greatest literary man whom that age produced, let us glance at the principal points in which his view of landscape differs from that of the mediævals.

I shall not endeavor now, as I did with Homer and Dante, to give a complete analysis of all the feelings which appear to be traceable in Scott's allusions to landscape scenery,—for this would require a volume,—but only to indicate the main points of differing character between his temper and Dante's. Then we will examine in detail, not the landscape of literature, but that of painting, which must, of course, be equally, or even in a higher degree, characteristic of the age.

And, first, observe Scott's habit of looking at
nature neither as dead, or merely material, in
the way that Homer regards it, nor as altered
by his own feelings, in the way that Keats and
Tennyson regard it, but as having an animation
and pathos of *its own*, wholly irrespective of
human presence or passion,—an animation
which Scott loves and sympathizes with, as he
would with a fellow-creature, forgetting himself
altogether, and subduing his own humanity before what seems to him the power of the landscape.

> "Yon lonely thorn,—would he could tell
> The changes of his parent dell,
> Since he, so gray and stubborn now,
> Waved in each breeze a sapling bough!
> Would he could tell, how deep the shade
> A thousand mingled branches made,
> How broad the shadows of the oak,
> How clung the rowan to the rock,
> And through the foliage showed his head,
> With narrow leaves and berries red!"

Scott does not dwell on the gray stubbornness of
the thorn, because he himself is at that moment
disposed to be dull, or stubborn; neither on the
cheerful peeping forth of the rowan, because he
himself is at that moment cheerful or curious:
but he perceives them both with the kind of interest that he would take in an old man, or a

climbing boy; forgetting himself, in sympathy with either age or youth.

> " And from the grassy slope he sees
>   The Greta flow to meet the Tees,
>   Where issuing from her darksome bed,
>   She caught the morning's eastern red,
>   And through the softening vale below
>   Rolled her bright waves in rosy glow,
>   All blushing to her bridal bed,
>   Like some shy maid, in convent bred;
>   While linnet, lark, and blackbird gay
>   Sing forth her nuptial roundelay."

Is Scott, or are the persons of his story, gay at this moment? Far from it. Neither Scott nor Risingham are happy, but the Greta is: and Scott's sympathy is ready for the Greta, on the instant.

Observe, therefore, this is not *pathetic* fallacy; for there is no passion in *Scott* which alters nature. It is not the lover's passion, making him think the larkspurs are listening for his lady's foot; it is not the miser's passion, making him think that dead leaves are falling coins; but it is an inherent and continual habit of thought, which Scott shares with the moderns in general, being, in fact, nothing else than the instinctive sense which men must have of the Divine presence, not formed into distinct belief. In the Greek it created, as we saw, the faithfully be-

lieved gods of the elements: in Dante and the
mediævals, it formed the faithfully believed angelic presence: in the modern, it creates no perfect form, does not apprehend distinctly any
Divine being or operation; but only a dim,
slightly credited animation in the natural object,
accompanied with great interest and affection
for it.   This feeling is quite universal with us,
only varying in depth according to the greatness
of the heart that holds it; and in Scott, being
more than usually intense, and accompanied with
infinite affection and quickness of sympathy, it
enables him to conquer all tendencies to the
pathetic fallacy, and, instead of making Nature
anywise subordinate to himself, he makes himself subordinate to *her*—follows her lead simply
—does not venture to bring his own cares and
thoughts into her pure and quiet presence—
paints her in her simple and universal truth,
adding no result of momentary passion or fancy,
and appears, therefore, at first shallower than
other poets, being in reality wider and healthier.
"What am I," he says continually, "that I
should trouble this sincere nature with my
thoughts ? I happen to be feverish and depressed, and I could see a great many sad and
strange things in those waves and flowers; but I
have no business to see such things.   Gay
Greta ! sweet harebells! *you* are not sad nor

strange to most people; you are but bright water and blue blossoms; you shall not be anything else to me, except that I cannot help thinking you are a little alive,—no one can help thinking that." And thus, as Nature is bright, serene, or gloomy, Scott takes her temper, and paints her as she is; nothing of himself being ever intruded, except that far-away Eolian tone, of which he is unconscious; and sometimes a stray syllable or two, like that about Blackford Hill, distinctly stating personal feeling, but all the more modestly for that distinctness, and for the clear consciousness that it is not the chiming brook, nor the cornfields, that are sad, but only the boy that rests by them; so returning on the instant to reflect, in all honesty, the image of Nature as she is meant by all to be received; nor that in fine words, but in the first that come; nor with comment of far-fetched thoughts, but with easy thoughts, such as all sensible men ought to have in such places, only spoken sweetly; and evidently also with an undercurrent of more profound reflection, which here and there murmurs for a moment, and which I think, if we choose, we may continually pierce down to, and drink deeply from, but which Scott leaves us to seek, or shun, at our pleasure.

And in consequence of this unselfishness and humility, Scott's enjoyment of Nature is incomparably greater than that of any other poet I know. All the rest carry their cares to her, and begin maundering in her ears about their own affairs. Tennyson goes out on a furzy common, and sees it is calm autumn sunshine, but it gives him no pleasure. He only remembers that it is

> " Dead calm in that noble breast
> Which heaves but with the heaving deep."

He sees a thundercloud in the evening, and *would* have " doted and pored " on it, but cannot, for fear it should bring the ship bad weather. Keats drinks the beauty of Nature violently; but has no more real sympathy with her than he has with a bottle of claret. His palate is fine; but he " bursts joy's grape against it," gets nothing but misery, and a bitter taste of dregs out of his desperate draught.

Byron and Shelley are nearly the same, only with less truth of perception, and even more troublesome selfishness. Wordsworth is more like Scott, and understands how to be happy, but yet cannot altogether rid himself of the sense that he is a philosopher, and ought always to be saying something wise. He has also a vague notion that Nature would not be able to get on well without Wordsworth; and finds a considerable part of his pleasure in looking at himself, as well as at her. But with Scott the love is entirely humble and unselfish. "I, Scott, am nothing, and less than nothing; but these crags, and heaths, and clouds, how great they are, how lovely, how for ever to be beloved, only for their own silent, thoughtless sake!"

This pure passion for nature in its abstract being, is still increased in its intensity by the two elements above taken notice of,—the love of antiquity, and the love of color and beautiful form, mortified in our streets, and seeking for food in the wilderness and the ruin: both feelings, observe, instinctive in Scott from his childhood, as everything that makes a man great is always.

> "And well the lonely infant knew
> Recesses where the wallflower grew,
> And honeysuckle loved to crawl,
> Up the long crag and ruined wall.
> I deemed such nooks the sweetest shade
> The sun in all its round surveyed."

Not that these could have been instinctive in a child in the Middle Ages. The sentiments of a people increase or diminish in intensity from generation to generation,—every disposition of the parents affecting the frame of the mind in their offspring: the soldier's child is born to be yet more a soldier, and the politician's to be still more a politician; even the slightest colors of sentiment and affection are transmitted to the heirs of life; and the crowning expression of the mind of a people is given when some infant of highest capacity, and sealed with the impress of this national character, is born where providential circumstances permit the full development of the powers it has received straight from Heaven, and the passions which it has inherited from its fathers.

This love of ancientness, and that of natural beauty, associate themselves also in Scott with the love of liberty, which was indeed at the root even of all his Jacobite tendencies in politics. For, putting aside certain predilections about landed property, and family name, and " gentlemanliness" in the club sense of the word,—respecting which I do not now inquire whether they were weak or wise,—the main element which makes Scott like Cavaliers better than Puritans is, that he thinks the former *free* and *masterful* as well as loyal; and the latter *formal* and *slavish.* He is loyal, not so much in respect for law, as in unselfish love for the king; and his sympathy is quite as ready for any active borderer who breaks the law, or fights the king, in what Scott thinks a generous way, as for the king himself. Rebellion of a rough, free, and bold kind he is always delighted by; he only objects to rebellion on principle and in form: bareheaded and open-throated treason he will abet to any extent, but shrinks from it in a peaked hat and starched collar: nay, politically, he only delights in kingship itself, because he looks upon it as the head and centre of liberty; and thinks that, keeping hold of a king's hand, one may get rid of the cramps and fences of law; and that the people may be governed by the whistle, as a Highland clan on the open hill-side, instead of being shut up into hurdled folds or hedged fields, as sheep or cattle left masterless.

And thus nature becomes dear to Scott in a threefold way: dear to him, first, as containing those remains or memories of the past, which he cannot find in cities, and giving hope of Prætorian mound or knight's grave, in every green slope and shade of its desolate places;—dear, secondly, in its moorland liberty, which has for him just as high a charm as the fenced garden had for the mediæval:

> " For I was wayward, bold, and wild,
>   A self-willed imp—a grandame's child;
>   But, half a plague, and half a jest,
>   Was still endured, beloved, caressed:
>   For me, thus nurtured, dost thou ask
>   The classic poet's well-conned task ?
>   Nay, Erskine, nay. On the wild hill
>   Let the wild heathbell flourish still;
>   Cherish the tulip, prune the vine;
>   But freely let the woodbine twine,
>   And leave untrimmed the eglantine;"

—and dear to him, finally, in that perfect beauty,
denied alike in cities and in men, for which
every modern heart had begun at last to thirst,
and Scott's, in its freshness and power, of all
men's, most earnestly.

And in this love of beauty, observe, that (as I
said we might except) the love of *color* is a leading element, his healthy mind being incapable of
losing, under any modern false teaching, its joy
in brilliancy of hue. Though not so subtle a
colorist as Dante, which, under the circumstances of the age, he could not be, he depends
quite as much upon color for his power or pleasure. And, in general, if he does not mean to say
much about things, the *one* character which he
will give is color, using it with the most perfect
mastery and faithfulness, up to the point of possible modern perception. For instance, if he
has a sea-storm to paint in a single line, he does
not, as a feebler poet would probably have done,
use any expression about the temper or form of
the waves; does not call them angry or mountain-
ous. He is content to strike them out with two
dashes of Tintoret's favorite colors:

> "*The blackening wave is edged with white;*"
> To inch and rock the seamews fly."

There is no form in this. Nay, the main virtue
of it is, that it gets rid of all form. The dark

raging of the sea—what form has that? But
out of the cloud of its darkness those lightning
flashes of the foam, coming at their terrible intervals—you need no more.

Again: where he has to describe tents mingled among oaks, he says nothing about the form
of either tent or tree, but only gives the two
strokes of color:

> " Thousand pavilions, *white as snow*,
> *Chequered* the borough moor below,
> Oft giving way, where still there stood
> Some relics of the old oak wood,
> That darkly huge did intervene,
> *And tamed the glaring white with green.*"

Again: of tents at Flodden:

> " Next morn the Baron climbed the tower,
> To view, afar, the Scottish power,
> Encamped on Flodden edge.
> The white pavilions made a show,
> Like remnants of the winter snow,
> Along the dusky ridge."

Again: of trees mingled with dark rocks:

> " Until, where Teith's young waters roll
> Betwixt him and a wooded knoll,
> That graced the *sable* strath with *green*,
> The chapel of St. Bride was seen."

Again: there is hardly any form, only smoke

and color in his celebrated description of Edinburgh:

> " The wandering eye could o'er it go,
>   And mark the distant city glow
>   With gloomy splendor red;
>   For on the smoke-wreaths, huge and slow,
>   That round her sable turrets flow,
>   The morning beams were shed,
>   And tinged them with a lustre proud,
>   Like that which streaks a thunder-cloud.
>   Such dusky grandeur clothed the height,
>   Where the huge castle holds its state,
>   And all the steep slope down,
>   Whose ridgy back heaves to the sky,
>   Piled deep and massy, close and high,
>   Mine own romantic town!
>   But northward far with purer blaze,
>   On Ochil mountains fell the rays,
>   And as each heathy top they kissed,
>   It gleamed a purple amethyst.
>   Yonder the shores of Fife you saw ;
>   Here Preston Bay and Berwick Law:
>   And, broad between them rolled,
>   The gallant Frith the eye might note,
>   Whose islands on its bosom float,
>   Like emeralds chased in gold."

I do not like to spoil a fine passage by italicizing it; but observe, the only hints at form, given throughout, are in the somewhat vague words, "ridgy," "massy," "close," and "high;" the whole being still more obscured by modern mystery, in its most tangible form of smoke.

But the *colors* are all definite; note the rainbow
band of them—gloomy or dusky red, sable (pure
black), amethyst (pure purple), green, and gold
—a noble chord throughout; and then, moved
doubtless less by the smoky than the amethys-
tine part of the group,

> " Fitz Eustace' heart felt closely pent,
>   The spur he to his charger lent,
>   And raised his bridle hand.
> And making demivolte in air,
> Cried, 'Where's the coward would not dare
>   To fight for such a land ?' "

I need not multiply examples: the reader can
easily trace for himself, through verse familiar to
us all, the force of these color instincts. I will
therefore add only two passages, not so completely known by heart as most of the poems in
which they occur.

> " 'Twas silence all.   He laid him down
>   Where purple heath profusely strown,
>   And throatwort, with its azure bell,
>   And moss and thyme his cushion swell.
> There, spent with toil, he listless eyed
> The course of Greta's playful tide;
> Beneath her banks, now eddying dun,
> Now brightly gleaming to the sun,
> As, dancing over rock and stone,
> In yellow light her currents shone,
> Matching in hue the favorite gem
> Of Albin's mountain diadem.

> Then tired to watch the current play,
> He turned his weary eyes away
> To where the bank opposing showed
> Its huge square cliffs through shaggy wood.
> One, prominent above the rest,
> Reared to the sun its pale gray breast;
> Around its broken summit grew
> The hazel rude, and sable yew;
> A thousand varied lichens dyed
> Its waste and weather-beaten side;
> And round its rugged basis lay,
> By time or thunder rent away,
> Fragments, that, from its frontlet torn,
> Were mantled now by verdant ' thorn.' "

Note, first, what an exquisite chord of color is given in the succession of this passage. It begins with purple and blue; then passes to gold, or cairngorm color (topaz color); then to *pale gray*, through which the yellow passes into black; and the black, through broken dyes of lichen, into green. Note, secondly,—what is indeed so manifest throughout Scott's landscape as hardly to need pointing out,—the love of rocks, and true understanding of their colors and characters, opposed as it is in every conceivable way to Dante's hatred and misunderstanding of them.

I have already traced, in various places, most of the causes of this great difference: namely, first, the ruggedness of northern temper (compare

§ 8. of the chapter on the Nature of Gothic in the Stones of Venice); then the really greater beauty of the northern rocks, as noted when we were speaking of the Apennine limestone; then the need of finding beauty among them, if it were to be found anywhere,—no well-arranged colors being any more to be seen in dress, but only in rock lichens; and, finally, the love of irregularity, liberty, and power, springing up in glorious opposition to laws of prosody, fashion, and the five orders.

The other passage I have to quote is still more interesting; because it has *no form* in it *at all* except in one word (chalice), but wholly composes its imagery either of color, or of that delicate half-believed life which we have seen to be so important an element in modern landscape.

> " The summer dawn's reflected hue
> *To purple changed Loch Katrine blue ;*
> Mildly and soft the western breeze
> Just kissed the lake ; just stirred the trees ;
> *And the pleased lake, like maiden coy,*
> *Trembled, but dimpled not, for joy ;*
> The mountain-shadows on her breast
> Were neither broken nor at rest;
> In bright uncertainty they lie,
> Like future joys to Fancy's eye.
> The water-lily to the light
> Her chalice reared of silver bright:

> The doe awoke, and to the lawn,
> Begemmed with dew-drops, led her fawn;
> The gray mist left the mountain side;
> The torrent showed its glistening pride;
> Invisible in fleckèd sky,
> The lark sent down her revelry;
> The blackbird and the speckled thrush
> Good-morrow gave from brake and bush;
> In answer cooed the cushat dove
> Her notes of peace, and rest, and love."

Two more considerations are, however, suggested by the above passage. The first, that the love of natural history, excited by the continual attention now given to all wild landscape, heightens reciprocally the interest of that landscape, and becomes an important element in Scott's description, leading him to finish, down to the minutest speckling of breast, and slightest shade of attributed emotion, the portraiture of birds and animals; in strange opposition to Homer's slightly named "sea-crows, who have care of the works of the sea," and Dante's singing-birds, of undefined species. Compare carefully a passage, too long to be quoted,—the 2nd and 3rd stanzas of canto VI. of Rokeby.

The second, and the last point I have to note, is Scott's habit of drawing a slight *moral* from every scene, just enough to excuse to his conscience his want of definite religious feeling; and that this slight moral is almost always melancholy. Here he has stopped short without entirely expressing it—

> " The mountain shadows
> .   .   .   lie
> Like future joys to Fancy's eye."

His completed thought would be, that those future joys, like the mountain shadows, were never to be attained. It occurs fully uttered in many other places. He seems to have been constantly rebuking his own wordly pride and vanity, but never purposefully:

> " The foam-globes on her eddies ride,
> Thick as the schemes of human pride
> That down life's current drive amain,
> As frail, as frothy, and as vain."

> " Foxglove, and nightshade, side by side,
> Emblems of punishment and pride."

> " Her dark eye flashed ; she paused and sighed ;—
> ' Ah, what have I to do with pride !'"

And hear the thought he gathers from the sunset (noting first the Turnerian color,—as usual, its principal element) :

> " The sultry summer day is done.
> The western hills have hid the sun,
> But mountain peak and village spire
> Retain reflection of his fire.
> Old Barnard's towers are purple still,
> To those that gaze from Toller Hill ;

> Distant and high the tower of Bowes
> Like steel upon the anvil glows ;
> And Stanmore's ridge, behind that lay,
> Rich with the spoils of parting day,
> In crimson and in gold arrayed,
> Streaks yet awhile the closing shade ;
> Then slow resigns to darkening heaven
> The tints which brighter hours had given.
> Thus, aged men, full loth and slow,
> The vanities of life forego,
> And count their youthful follies o'er
> Till Memory lends her light no more."

That is, as far as I remember, one of the most
finished pieces of sunset he has given ; and it
has a woful moral ; yet one which, with Scott, is
inseparable from the scene.

Hark, again :

> " ' Twere sweet to mark the setting day
> On Bourhope's lonely top decay ;
> And, as it faint and feeble died
> On the broad lake and mountain side,
> To say, ' Thus pleasures fade away ;
> Youth, talents, beauty, thus decay,
> And leave us dark, forlorn, and gray."

And again, hear Bertram :

> " Mine be the eve of tropic sun :
> With disk like battle target red,
> He rushes to his burning bed,
> Dyes the wide wave with bloody light,
> Then sinks at once ; and all is night."

In all places of this kind, where a passing thought is suggested by some external scene that thought is at once a slight and sad one. Scott's deeper moral sense is marked in the *conduct* of his stories, and in casual reflections or exclamations arising out of their plot, and therefore sincerely uttered ; as that of Marmion :

> " Oh, what a tangled web we weave,
>   When first we practise to deceive !"

But the reflections which are founded, not on events, but on scenes, are, for the most part, shallow, partly insincere, and, as far as sincere, sorrowful. This habit of ineffective dreaming and moralizing over passing scenes, of which the earliest type I know is given in Jaques, is, as aforesaid, usually the satisfaction made to our modern consciences for the want of a sincere acknowledgment of God in nature : and Shakspeare has marked it as the characteristic of a mind " compact of jars."

In the reading of a great poem, in the hearing of a noble oration, it is the subject of the writer and not his skill,—his passion, not his power, on which our minds are fixed. We see as he sees, but we see not him. We become part of him, feel with him, judge, behold with him ; but we

think of him as little as of ourselves. Do we
think of Æschylus while we wait on the silence
of Cassandra, or of Shakspeare while we listen to
the wailing of Lear ? Not so. The power of
the masters is known by their self-annihilation.
It is commensurate with the degree in which
they themselves appear not in their work. The
harp of the minstrel is untruly touched, if his
own glory is all that it truly records. Every
great writer may be at once known by his guiding
the mind far from himself to the beauty which is
not of his creation, and the knowledge which is
past his finding out.

I admit two orders of poets, but no third ;
and by these two orders I mean the Creative
(Shakspeare, Homer, Dante), and Reflective or
Perceptive (Wordsworth, Keats, Tennyson).
But both of these must be *first*-rate in their
range, though their range is different ; and with
poetry second-rate in *quality* no one ought to be
allowed to trouble mankind. There is quite
enough of the best,—much more than we can
ever read or enjoy in the length of a life ; and
it is a literal wrong or sin in any person to encumber us with inferior work. I have no patience with apologies made by young pseudo-
poets, " that they believe there is *some* good in
what they have written : that they hope to do

better in time," etc. *Some* good! If there is
not *all* good, there is no good. If they ever
hope to do better, why do they trouble us now?
Let them rather courageously burn all they have
done, and wait for the better days. There are
few men, ordinarily educated, who in moments
of strong feeling could not strike out a poetical
thought, and afterwards polish it so as to be
presentable. But men of sense know better
than so to waste their time; and those who sincerely love poetry, know the touch of the master's hand on the chords too well to fumble
among them after him. Nay more than this;
all inferior poetry is an injury to the good, inasmuch as it takes away the freshness of rhymes,
blunders upon and gives a wretched commonalty
to good thoughts; and, in general, adds to the
weight of human weariness in a most woful and
culpable manner. There are few thoughts likely
to come across ordinary men, which have not
already been expressed by greater men in the
best possible way, and it is a wiser, more generous, more noble thing to remember and point
out the perfect words, than to invent poorer
ones, wherewith to encumber temporarily the
world.

Keats, describing a wave, breaking, out at sea,
says of it—

"Down whose green back the short-lived foam, all hoar,
  Bursts gradual, with a wayward indolence."

That is quite perfect, as an example of the modern manner. The idea of the peculiar action with which foam rolls down a long, large wave could not have been given by any other words so well as by this " wayward indolence." But Homer would never have written, never thought of, such words. He could not by any possibility have lost sight of the great fact that the wave from the beginning to the end of it, do what it might, was still nothing else than salt water ; and that salt water could not be either wayward or indolent. He will call the waves " over-roofed," " full-charged," " monstrous," " compact-black," " dark-clear," " violet-colored," " wine-colored," and so on. But every one of these epithets is descriptive of pure physical nature. " Over-roofed " is the term he invariably uses of anything—rock, house, or wave—that nods over at the brow ; the other terms need no explanation ; they are as accurate and intense in truth as words can be, but they never show the slightest feeling of anything animated in the ocean. Black or clear, monstrous or violet-colored, cold salt water it is always, and nothing but that.

And thus, in full, there are four classes; the men who feel nothing, and therefore see truly;

the men who feel strongly, think weakly, and see untruly (second order of poets); the men who feel strongly, think strongly, and see truly (first order of poets); and the men who, strong as human creatures can be, are yet submitted to influences stronger than they, and see in a sort untruly, because what they see is inconceivably above them. This last is the usual condition of prophetic inspiration.

I separate these classes, in order that their character may be clearly understood; but of course they are united each to the other by imperceptible transitions, and the same mind, according to the influences to which it is subjected, passes at different times into the various states. Still, the difference between the great and less man is, on the whole, chiefly in this point of *alterability*. That is to stay, the one knows too much, and perceives and feels too much of the past and future, and of all things beside and around that which immediately affects him, to be in any wise shaken by it. His mind is made up; his thoughts have an accustomed current; his ways are steadfast; it is not this or that new sight which will at once unbalance him. He is tender to impression at the surface, like a rock with deep moss upon it; but there is too much mass of him to be moved. The smaller man, with the same degree of sen-

sibility, is at once carried off his feet; he wants
to do something he did not want to do before;
he views all the universe in a new light through
his tears; he is gay or enthusiastic, melancholy
or passionate, as things come and go to him.
Therefore the high creative poet might even be
thought, to a great extent, impassive (as shallow people think Dante stern), receiving indeed
all feelings to the full, but having a great centre of reflection and knowledge in which he
stands serene, and watches the feeling, as it
were, from far off.

Dante, in his most intense moods, has entire
command of himself, and can look around calmly,
at all moments, for the image or the word that
will best tell what he sees to the upper or lower
world.   But Keats and Tennyson, and the poets
of the second order, are generally themselves
subdued by the feelings under which they
write, or at least, write as choosing to be so,
and therefore admit certain expressions and
modes of thought which are in some sort diseased or false.

Now so long as we see that the *feeling* is true,
we pardon, or are even pleased by, the confessed
fallacy of sight which it induces.   But the moment the mind of the speaker becomes cold,
that moment every such expression becomes untrue, as being for ever untrue in the external

facts. And there is no greater baseness in literature than the habit of using these metaphorical expressions in cool blood. An inspired writer, in full impetuosity of passion, may speak wisely and truly of " raging waves of the sea, foaming out their own shame;" but it is only the basest writer who cannot speak of the sea without talking of " raging waves," " remorseless floods," " ravenous billows," etc.; and it is one of the signs of the highest power in a writer to check all such habits of thought, and to keep his eyes fixed firmly on the *pure fact*, out of which if any feeling comes to him or his reader, he knows it must be a true one.

To keep to the waves, I forget who it is who represents a man in despair, desiring that his body may be cast into the sea,

> " *Whose changing mound, and foam that passed away,*
> Might mock the eye that questioned where I lay."

Observe, there is not a single false, or even overcharged, expression. " Mound " of the sea wave is perfectly simple and true; " changing " is as familiar as may be; " foam that passed away," strictly literal; and the whole line descriptive of the reality with a degree of accuracy which I know not any other verse, in the range of poetry, that altogether equals. For most people have not a distinct idea of the clumsiness and massiveness of a large wave. The word "wave" is used too generally of ripples and breakers, and bendings in light drapery or grass; it does not by itself convey a perfect image. But the word "mound" is heavy, large, dark, definite; there is no mistaking the kind of wave meant, nor missing the sight of it. Then the term "changing" has a peculiar force also. Most people think of waves as rising and falling. But if they look at the sea carefully, they will perceive that the waves do not rise and fall. They change. Change both place and form, but they do not fall; one wave goes on, and on, and still on; now lower, now higher, now tossing its mane like a horse, now building itself together like a wall, now shaking, now steady, but still the same wave, till at last it seems struck by something, and changes, one knows not how, —becomes another wave.

The close of the line insists on this image, and paints it still more perfectly,—"foam that passed away." Not merely melting, disappearing, but passing on, out of sight, on the career of the wave. Then, having put the absolute ocean fact as far as he may before our eyes, the poet leaves us to feel about it as we may, and to trace for ourselves the opposite fact, the image of the green mounds that do not change, and the white and written stones that do not pass away; and thence to follow out also the associated images of the calm life with the quiet grave, and the despairing life with the fading foam;—

> " Let no man move his bones."

" As for Samaria, her king is cut off like the foam upon the water."

But nothing of this is actually told or pointed out, and the expressions, as they stand, are perfectly severe and accurate, utterly uninfluenced by the firmly governed emotion of the writer. Even the word "mock" is hardly an exception, as it may stand merely for "deceive" or "defeat," without implying any impersonation of the waves.

It may be well, perhaps, to give an instance to show the peculiar dignity possessed by all passages which limit their expression to the pure fact, and leave the hearer to gather what he can from it.   Here is a notable one from the Iliad.   Helen, looking from the Scæan gate of Troy over the Grecian host, and telling Priam the names of its captains, says at last:—

" I see all the other dark-eyed Greeks; but two I cannot see,—Castor and Pollux,—whom one mother bore with me.   Have they not followed from fair Lacedæmon, or have they indeed come in their sea-wandering ships, but now will not enter into the battle of men, fearing the shame and the scorn that is in me?"

Then Homer:—

"So she spoke. But them, already, the life-giving earth possessed, there in Lacedæmon, in the dear fatherland."

Note, here, the high poetical truth carried to the extreme. The poet has to speak of the earth in sadness, but he will not let the sadness affect or change his thoughts of it. No; though Castor and Pollux be dead, yet the earth is our mother still, fruitful, life-giving. These are the facts of the thing. I see nothing else than these. Make what you will of them.

Take another very notable instance from Casimir de la Vigne's terrible ballad, "La Toilette de Constance." I must quote a few lines out of it here and there, to enable the reader who has not the book by him to understand its close.

> " Vite, Anna, vite; au miroir
>   Plus viti, Anna.   L'heure s'avance,
>   Et je vais au bal ce soir
>   Chez l'ambassadeur de France.
>
> Y pensez vous, ils sont fanés, ces nœuds,
>   Ils sont d'hier, mon Dieu, comme tout passe!
> Que du réseau qui retient mes cheveux
>   Les glands d'azur retombent avec grâce.
>
> Plus haut!   Plus bas!   Vous ne comprenez rien!
>   Que sur mon front ce saphir étincelle:
> Vous me piquez, mal-adroite.   Ah, c'est bien,
>   Bien,—chére Anna! Je t'aime, je suis belle.

Celui qu'en vain je voudrais oublier
   (Anna, ma robe) il y sera, j'espére.
(Ah, fi profane, est-ce là mon collier?
    Quoi! ces grains d'or bénits per le Saint Père!)
Il y sera; Dieu, s'il pressait ma main
   En y pensant, á peine je respire:
Père Anselmo doit m'entendre demain,
   Comment ferai-je, Anna, pour tout lui dire?

        Vite, in coup d'œil au miroir,
          Le dernier. ——— J'ai l'assurance
        Qu'on va m'adorer ce soir
          Chez l'ambassadeur de France.

Près du foyer, Constance s'admirait.
   Dieu! sur sa robe il vole une étincelle!
Au feu. Courez; Quand l'espoir l'enivrait
   Tout perdre ainsi! Quoi! Mourir,—et si belle!
L'horrible feu ronge avec volupté
   Ses bras, son sein, et l'entoure, et s'élève,
Et sans pitie dévore sa beauté,
   Ses dixhuit ans, hélas, et son doux réve!

        Adieu, bal, plaisir, amour!
          On disait, Pauvre Constance!
        Et on dansait, jusqu'au jour,
          Chez l'ambassadeur de France."

Yes, that is the fact of it. Right or wrong, the poet does not say. What you may think about it, he does not know. He has nothing to do with that. There lie the ashes of the dead girl in her chamber. There they danced. till the morning, at the Ambassador's of France. Make what you will of it.

If the reader will look through the ballad, of which I have quoted only about the third part he will find that there is not, from beginning to end of it, a single poetical (so called) expression, except in one stanza.   The girl speaks as simple prose as may be; there is not a word she would not have actually used as she was dressing. The poet stands by, impassive as a statue, recording her words just as they come.   At last the doom seizes her, and in the very presence of death, for an instant, his own emotions conquer him.   He records no longer the facts only, but the facts as they seem to him.   The fire gnaws with *voluptuousness—without pity.*   It is soon past.   The fate is fixed for ever; and he retires into his pale and crystalline atmosphere of truth.   He closes all with the calm veracity,

"They said, ' Poor Constance!' "

Now in this there is the exact type of the consummate poetical temperament.   For, be it clearly and constantly remembered, that the greatness of a poet depends upon the two faculties, acuteness of feeling, and command of it. A poet is great, first in proportion to the strength of his passion, and then, that strength being granted, in proportion to his government of it; there being, however, always a point beyond which it would be inhuman and monstrous if he pushed this government, and, therefore, a point at which all feverish and wild fancy becomes just and true. Thus the destruction of the kingdom of Assyria cannot be contemplated firmly by a prophet of Israel. The fact is too great, too wonderful. It overthrows him, dashes him into a confused element of dreams. All the world is, to his stunned thought, full of strange voices. "Yea, the fir-trees rejoice at thee, and the cedars of Lebanon, saying, 'Since thou art gone down to the grave, no feller is come up against us.'" So, still more, the thought of the presence of Deity cannot be borne without this great astonishment. "The mountains and the hills shall break forth before you into singing, and all the trees of the fields shall clap their hands."

But by how much this feeling is noble when it is justified by the strength of its cause, by so much it is ignoble when there is not cause enough for it; and beyond all other ignobleness is the mere affectation of it, in hardness of heart. Simply bad writing may almost always, as above noticed, be known by its adoption of these fanciful metaphorical expressions, as a sort of current coin; yet there is even a worse, at least a more harmful, condition of writing than this, in which such expressions are not ignorantly and feelinglessly caught up, but, by some master, skilful in handling, yet insincere, deliberately wrought out with chill and studied fancy; as if we should try to make an old lava stream look red-hot again, by covering it with dead leaves, or white-hot, with hoar-frost.

When Young is lost in veneration, as he dwells on the character of a truly good and holy man, he permits himself for a moment to be over-borne by the feeling so far as to exclaim—

> " Where shall I find him? angels, tell me where.
> You know him; he is near you: point him out.
> Shall I see glories beaming from his brow,
> Or trace his footsteps by the rising flowers?"

This emotion had a worthy cause, and is thus true and right. But now hear the cold-hearted Pope say to a shepherd girl—

> " Where'er you walk, cool gales shall fan the glade!
> Trees, where you sit, shall crowd into a shade;
> Your praise the birds shall chant in every grove,
> And winds shall waft it to the powers above.
> But would you sing, and rival Orpheus' strain,
> The wandering forests soon should dance again;
> The moving mountains hear the powerful call,
> And headlong streams hang, listening, in their fall."

This is not, nor could it for a moment be mistaken for, the language of passion. It is simple falsehood, uttered by hypocrisy; definite absurdity, rooted in affectation, and coldly as-serted in the teeth of nature and fact. Passion will indeed go far in deceiving itself; but it must be a strong passion, not the simple wish of a lover to tempt his mistress to sing. Compare a very closely parallel passage in Wordsworth, in which the lover has lost his mistress:

"Three years had Barbara in her grave been laid,
  When thus his moan he made:—

'Oh, move, thou cottage, from behind yon oak,
  Or let the ancient tree uprooted lie,
That in some other way yon smoke
  May mount into the sky.
If still behind yon pine-tree's ragged bough,
  Headlong, the waterfall must come,
  Oh, let it, then, be dumb—
Be anything, sweet stream, but that which thou art now.'"

Here is a cottage to be moved, if not a mountain, and a waterfall to be silent, if it is not to hang listening; but with what different relation to the mind that contemplates them! Here, in the extremity of its agony, the soul cries out wildly for relief, which at the same moment it partly knows to be impossible, but partly believes possible, in a vague impression that a miracle *might* be wrought to give relief even to a less sore distress,—that nature is kind, and God is kind, and that grief is strong; it knows not well what *is* possible to such grief. To silence a stream, to move a cottage wall,—one might think it could do as much as that!

I believe these instances are enough to illustrate the main point I insist upon respecting the
pathetic fallacy,—that so far as it *is* a fallacy, it
is always the sign of a morbid state of mind, and
comparatively of a weak one.   Even in the most
inspired prophet it is a sign of the incapacity of
his human sight or thought to bear what has
been revealed to it.   In ordinary poetry, if it is
found in the thoughts of the poet himself, it is
at once a sign of his belonging to the inferior
school; if in the thoughts of the characters imagined by him, it is right or wrong according to
the genuineness of the emotion from which it
springs; always, however, implying necessarily
some degree of weakness in the character.

Take two most exquisite instances from master hands.   The Jessy of Shenstone, and the
Ellen of Wordsworth, have both been betrayed
and deserted.   Jessy, in the course of her most
touching complaint, says:

" If through the garden's flowery tribes I stray,
    Where bloom the jasmines that could once allure,
 ' Hope not to find delight in us,' they say,
    ' For we are spotless, Jessy; we are pure.'"

Compare with this some of the words of Ellen:

" 'Ah, why,' said Ellen, sighing to herself,
 ' Why do not words, and kiss, and solemn pledge,
   And nature, that is kind in woman's breast,
   And reason, that in man is wise and good,
   And fear of Him who is a righteous Judge,—

Why do not these prevail for human life,
To keep two hearts together, that began
Their springtime with one love, and that have need
Of mutual pity and forgiveness, sweet
To grant, or be received; while that poor bird—
O, come and hear him! Thou who hast to me
Been faithless, hear him;—though a lowly creature,
One of God's simple children, that yet know not
The Universal Parent, *how* he sings!
As if he wished the firmament of heaven
Should listen, and give back to him the voice
Of his triumphant constancy and love.
The proclamation that he makes, how far
His darkness doth transcend our fickle light.' "

The perfection of both these passages, as far as regards truth and tenderness of imagination in the two poets, is quite insuperable. But, of the two characters imagined, Jessy is weaker than Ellen, exactly in so far as something appears to her to be in nature which is not. The flowers do not really reproach her. God meant them to comfort her, not to taunt her; they would do so if she saw them rightly.

Ellen, on the other hand, is quite above the slightest erring emotion. There is not the barest film of fallacy in all her thoughts. She reasons as calmly as if she did not feel. And, although the singing of the bird suggests to her the idea of its desiring to be heard in heaven, she does not for an instant admit any veracity in the thought. " As if," she says,—" I know he means nothing of the kind; but it does verily seem as if." The reader will find, by examining the rest of the poem, that Ellen's character is throughout consistent in this clear though passionate strength.

It then being, I hope, now made clear to the reader in all respects that the pathetic fallacy is powerful only so far as it is pathetic, feeble so far as it is fallacious, and, therefore, that the dominion of Truth is entire, over this, as over every other natural and just state of the human mind, we may go on to the subject for the dealing with which this prefatory inquiry became necessary; and why necessary, we shall see forthwith.*

---

* I cannot quit this subject without giving two more instances, both exquisite, of the pathetic fallacy, which I have just come upon, in Maude:

> " For a great speculation had fail'd;
> And ever he mutter'd and madden'd, and ever
>   wann'd with despair;
> And out he walk'd, when the wind like a broken
>   worldling wand,
> And the *flying gold of the ruin'd woodlands drove
>   thro' the air*."

> "There has fallen a splendid tear
>   From the passion-flower at the gate.
> *The red rose cries,   She is near, she is near!*'
>   *And the white rose weeps, ' She is late,'*
> *The larkspur listens, ' I hear, I hear!'*
>   *And the lily whispers, ' I wait.'*"

Very frequently things which appear to us ignoble are merely the simplicities of a pure and truthful age. When Juno beats Diana about the ears with her own quiver, for instance, we start at first, as if Homer could not have believed that they were both real goddesses. But what should Juno have done? Killed Diana with a look? Nay, she neither wished to do so, nor could she have done so, by the very faith of Diana's goddess-ship. Diana is as immortal as herself. Frowned Diana into submission? But Diana has come expressly to try conclusions with her, and will by no means be frowned into submission. Wounded her with a celestial lance? That sounds more poetical, but it is in reality partly more savage, and partly more absurd, than Homer. More savage, for it makes Juno more cruel, therefore less divine; and more absurd, for it only seems elevated in tone, because we use the word "celestial," which means nothing. What sort of a thing is a "celestial" lance? Not a wooden one. Of what then? Of moonbeams, or clouds, or mist. Well, therefore, Diana's arrows were of mist too; and her quiver, and herself, and Juno with her lance, and all, vanish into mist. Why not have said at once, if that is all you mean, that two mists met, and one drove the other back? That would have been rational and intelligible, but not to talk of celestial lances. Homer had no such misty fancy; he believed the two goddesses were there in true bodies, with true weapons, on the true earth; and still I ask what should Juno have done? Not beaten Diana? No; for it is un-lady-like. Un-English-lady-like, yes; but by no means un-Greek-lady-like, nor even un-natural-lady-like. If a modern lady does *not* beat her servant or her rival about the ears, it is oftener because she is too weak, or too proud, than because she is of purer mind than Homer's Juno. She will not strike them; but she will over-work the one or slander the other without pity; and Homer would not have thought that one whit more goddess-like than striking them with her one hand.

What, then, was actually the Greek god? In what way were these two ideas of human form, and divine power, credibly associated in the ancient heart, so as to become a subject of true faith, irrespective equally of fable, allegory, superstitious trust in stone, and demoniacal influence?

It seems to me that the Greek had exactly the same instinctive feeling about the elements that we have ourselves; that to Homer, as much as to Casimir de la Vigne, fire seemed ravenous and pitiless; to Homer, as much as to Keats, the sea-wave appeared wayward or idle, or whatever

else it may be to the poetical passion. The
Greek never removed his god out of nature at
all; never attempted for a moment to contradict
his instinctive sense that God was everywhere.
" The tree *is* glad," said he, " I know it is; I can
cut it down; no matter, there was a nymph in it.
The water *does* sing," said he; " I can dry it up;
but no matter, there was a naiad in it." But in
thus clearly defining his belief, observe, he threw
it entirely into a human form, and gave his faith
to nothing but the image of his own humanity.
What sympathy and fellowship he had, were always for the spirit *in* the stream, not for the
stream; always for the dryad *in* the wood, not
for the wood. Content with this human sympathy, he approached the actual waves and
woody fibres with no sympathy at all. The
spirit that ruled them, he received as a plain fact.
Them, also, ruled and material, he received as
plain facts; they, without their spirit, were dead
enough. A rose was good for scent, and a
stream for sound and coolness; for the rest, one
was no more than leaves, the other no more
than water; he could not make anything else of
them; and the divine power which was involved
in their existence, having been all distilled away
by him into an independent Flora or Thetis, the
poor leaves or waves were left, in mere cold
corporealness, to make the most of their being

discernibly red and soft, clear and wet, and un-acknowledged in any other power whatsoever.

Then, observe farther, the Greeks lived in the midst of the most beautiful nature, and were as familiar with blue sea, clear air, and sweet out-lines of mountain, as we are with brick walls, black smoke, and level fields. This perfect familiarity rendered all such scenes of natural beauty unexciting, if not indifferent to them, by lulling and overwearying the imagination as far as it was concerned with such things; but there was another kind of beauty which they found it required effort to obtain, and which, when thor-oughly obtained, seemed more glorious than any of this wild loveliness—the beauty of the human countenance and form. This, they perceived, could only be reached by continual exercise of virtue; and it was in Heaven's sight, and theirs, all the more beautiful because it needed this self-denial to obtain it. So they set themselves to reach this, and having gained it, gave it their principal thoughts, and set it off with beautiful dress as best they might. But making this their object, they were obliged to pass their lives in simple exercise and disciplined employments. Living wholesomely, giving themselves no fever fits, either by fasting or over-eating, constantly in the open air, and full of animal spirit and physical power, they became incapable of every morbid condition of mental emotion. Unhappy love, disappointed ambition, spiritual despondency, or any other disturbing sensation, had little power over the well-braced nerves, and healthy flow of the blood; and what bitterness might yet fasten on them was soon boxed or raced out of a boy, and spun or woven out of a girl, or danced out of both. They had indeed their sorrows, true and deep, but still, more like children's sorrows than ours, whether bursting into open cry of pain, or hid with shuddering under the veil, still passing over the soul as clouds do over heaven, not sullying it, not mingling with it;—darkening it perhaps long or utterly, but still not becoming one with it, and for the most part passing away in dashing rain of tears, and leaving the man unchanged; in nowise affecting, as our sorrow does, the whole tone of his thought and imagination thenceforward.

How far our melancholy may be deeper and wider than theirs, in its roots and view, and therefore nobler, we shall consider presently; but at all events, they had the advantage of us in being entirely free from all those dim and feverish sensations which result from unhealthy state of the body. I believe that a large amount of the dreamy and sentimental sadness, tendency to reverie, and general patheticalness of modern life results merely from derangement of stomach ; holding to the Greek life the same relation that the feverish night of an adult does to a child's sleep.

Farther. The human beauty, which, whether in its bodily being or in imagined divinity, had become, for the reasons we have seen, the principal object of culture and sympathy to these Greeks, was, in its perfection, eminently orderly, symmetrical, and tender. Hence, contemplating it constantly in this state, they could not but feel a proportionate fear of all that was disorderly, unbalanced, and rugged. Having trained their stoutest soldiers into a strength so delicate and lovely, that their white flesh, with their blood upon it, should look like ivory stained with purple ;* and having always around them, in the motion and majesty of this beauty, enough for the full employment of their imagination, they shrank with dread or hatred from all the ruggedness of lower nature,—from the wrinkled forest bark, the jagged hill-crest, and irregular, inorganic storm of sky ; looking to these for the most part as adverse powers, and taking pleasure only in such portions of the lower world as were at once conducive to the rest and health of the human frame, and in har mony with the laws of its gentler beauty.

---

* Iliad iv. 141.

I know many persons who have the purest taste in literature, and yet false taste in art, and it is a phenomenon which puzzles me not a little; but I have never known any one with false taste in books, and true taste in pictures. It is also of the greatest importance to you, not only for art's sake, but for all kinds of sake, in these days of book deluge, to keep out of the salt swamps of literature, and live on a little rocky island of your own, with a spring and a lake in it, pure and good. I cannot, of course, suggest the choice of your library to you, every several mind needs different books; but there are some books which we all need, and assuredly, if you read Homer,* Plato, Æschylus, Herodotus, Dante,† Shakspeare, and Spencer, as much as you ought, you will not require wide enlargement of shelves to right and left of them for purposes of perpetual study. Among modern books, avoid generally magazine and review literature. Sometimes it may contain a useful

---

* Chapman's, if not the original,

† Carey's or Cayley's, if not the original. I do not know which are the best translations of Plato. Herodotus and Æschylus can only be read in the original. It may seem strange that I name books like these for "beginners:" but all the greatest books contain food for all ages; and an intelligent and rightly bred youth or girl ought to enjoy much, even in Plato, by the time they are fifteen or sixteen.

abridgment or a wholesome piece of criticism;
but the chances are ten to one it will either
waste your time or mislead you. If you want to
understand any subject whatever, read the best
book upon it you can hear of ; not a review of
the book. If you don't like the first book you
try, seek for another; but do not hope ever to
understand the subject without pains, by a re-
viewer's help. Avoid especially that class of
literature which has a knowing tone; it is the
most poisonous of all. Every good book, or
piece of book, is full of admiration and awe ; it
may contain firm assertion, or stern satire, but
it never sneers coldly, nor asserts haughtily, and
it always leads you to reverence or love something with your whole heart. It is not always
easy to distinguish the satire of the venomous
race of books from the satire of the noble and pure
ones; but in general you may notice that the
cold-blooded Crustacean and Batrachian books
will sneer at sentiment; and the warm-blooded,
human books, at sin. Then, in general, the
more you can restrain your serious reading to
reflective or lyric poetry, history, and natural
history, avoiding fiction and the drama, the
healthier your mind will become. Of modern
poetry keep to Scott, Wordsworth, Keats,
Crabbe, Tennyson, the two Brownings, Lowell,
Longfellow, and Coventry Patmore, whose

" Angel in the House" is a most finished piece of writing, and the sweetest analysis we possess of quiet modern domestic feeling; while Mrs. Browning's " Aurora Leigh" is, as far as I know, the greatest poem which the century has produced in any language. Cast Coleridge at once aside, as sickly and useless; and Shelley, as shallow and verbose; Byron, until your taste is fully formed, and you are able to discern the magnificence in him from the wrong. Never read bad or common poetry, nor write any poetry yourself; there is, perhaps, rather too much than too little in the world already.

Of reflective prose, read chiefly, Bacon, Johnson, and Helps. Carlyle is hardly to be named as a writer for " beginners," because his teaching, though to some of us vitally necessary, may to others be hurtful. If you understand and like him, read him; if he offends you, you are not yet ready for him, and perhaps may never be so; at all events, give him up, as you would sea-bathing if you found it hurt you, till you are stronger. Of fiction, read Sir Charles Grandison, Scott's novels, Miss Edgeworth's, and, if you are a young lady, Madame de Genlis', the French Miss Edgeworth; making these, I mean, your constant companions. Of course you must, or will, read other books for amusement, once or twice; but you will find that these have an element of perpetuity in them, existing in nothing else of their kind; while their peculiar quietness and repose of manner will also be of the greatest value in teaching you to feel the same characters in art. Read little at a time trying to feel interest in little things, and reading not so much for the sake of the story as to get acquainted with the pleasant people into whose company these writers bring you. A common book will often give you much amusement, but it is only a noble book which will give you dear friends. Remember also that it is of less importance to you in your earlier years, that the books you read should be clever, than that they should be right. I do not mean oppressively or repulsively instructive; but that the thoughts they express should be just, and the feelings they excite generous. It is not necessary for you to read the wittiest or the most suggestive books: it is better, in general, to hear what is already known, and may be simply said. Much of the literature of the present day, though good to be read by persons of ripe age, has a tendency to agitate rather than confirm, and leaves its readers too frequently in a helpless or hopeless indignation, the worst possible state into which the mind of youth can be thrown. It may, indeed, become necessary for you, as you advance in life, to set your hand to things that need to be altered in the world, or apply your heart chiefly to what must be pitied in it, or condemned ; but, for a young person, the safest temper is one of reyerence, and the safest place one of obscurity. Certainly at present, and perhaps through all your life, your teachers are wisest when they make you content in quiet virtue, and that literature and art are best for you which point out, in common life and familiar things, the objects for hopeful labor, and for humble love.

MORALS AND RELIGION.

———◆———

Next to Sincerity, remember still,
Thou must resolve upon Integrity.
God will have all thou hast ; thy mind, thy will,
Thy thoughts, thy words, thy works.

GEORGE HERBER

MORALS AND RELIGION.

THE Bible is specifically distinguished from all
other early literature, by its delight in natural
imagery; and the dealings of God with his people
are calculated peculiarly to awaken this sensibility within them. Out of the monotonous
valley of Egypt they are instantly taken into the
midst of the mightiest mountain scenery in the
peninsula of Arabia; and that scenery is associated in their minds with the immediate manifestation and presence of the Divine Power; so that
mountains for ever afterwards become invested
with a peculiar sacredness in their minds; while
their descendants being placed in what was then
one of the loveliest districts upon the earth, full
of glorious vegetation, bounded on one side
by the sea, on the north by "that goodly mountain" Lebanon, on the south and east by deserts,
whose barrenness enhanced by their contrast
the sense of the perfection of beauty in their
own land, they became, by these means, and by

the touch of God's own hand upon their hearts, sensible to the appeal of natural scenery in a way in which no other people were at the time; and their literature is full of expressions, not only testifying a vivid sense of the power of nature over man, but showing that *sympathy with natural things themselves*, as if they had human souls, which is the especial characteristic of true love of the works of God. I intended to have insisted on this sympathy at greater length, but I found, only two or three days ago, much of what I had to say to you anticipated in a little book, unpretending, but full of interest, "The Lamp and the Lantern," by Dr. James Hamilton; and I will therefore only ask you to consider such expressions as that tender and glorious verse in Isaiah, speaking of the cedars on the mountains as rejoicing over the fall of the king of Assyria: "Yea, the fir-trees rejoice at thee, and the cedars of Lebanon, saying, Since *thou* art gone down to the grave, no feller is come up against us." See what sympathy there is here, as if with the very hearts of the trees themselves. So also in the words of Christ, in his personification of the lilies: "They toil not, neither do they spin." Consider such expressions as, "The sea saw that, and fled. Jordan was driven back. The mountains skipped like rams; and the little hills like lambs." Try to find anything in profane writing like this; and note farther that the whole book of Job appears to have been chiefly written and placed in the inspired volume in order to show the value of natural history, and its power on the human heart. I cannot pass by it without pointing out the evidences of the beauty of the country that Job inhabited.

Observe, first, it was an arable country. "The oxen were ploughing, and the asses feeding beside them." It was a pastoral country: his substance, besides camels and asses, was 7000 sheep. It was a mountain country, fed by streams descending from the high snows. "My brethren have dealt deceitfully as a brook, and as the stream of brooks they pass away; which are blackish by reason of the ice, and wherein the snow is hid: What time they wax warm they vanish: when it is hot they are consumed out of their place." Again: "If I wash myself with snow water, and make my hands never so clean." Again: "Drought and heat consume the snow waters." It was a rocky country, with forests and verdure rooted in the rocks. "His branch shooteth forth in his garden; his roots are wrapped about the heap, and seeth the place of stones." Again: "Thou shalt be in league with the stones of the field." It was a place visited, like the valleys of Switzerland, by convulsions

and falls of mountains. "Surely the mountain
falling cometh to nought and the rock is removed out of his place." "The waters wear the
stones: thou washest away the things which
grow out of the dust of the earth." "He re-
moveth the mountains and they know not: he
overturneth them in his anger." "He putteth
forth his hand upon the rock: he overturneth
the mountains by the roots; he cutteth out
rivers among the rocks." I have not time to go
farther into this; but you see Job's country was
one like your own, full of pleasant brooks and
rivers, rushing among the rocks, and of all other
sweet and noble elements of landscape. The
magnificent allusions to natural scenery throughout the book are therefore calculated to touch
the heart to the end of time.

Then at the central point of Jewish prosperity,
you have the first great naturalist the world ever
saw, Solomon, not permitted, indeed, to anticipate, in writing, the discoveries of modern times,
but so gifted as to show us that heavenly wisdom
is manifested as much in the knowledge of the
hyssop that springeth out of the wall as in
political and philosophical speculation.

The books of the Old Testament, as distinguished from all other early writings, are thus
prepared for an everlasting influence over
humanity; and, finally, Christ himself, setting

the concluding example to the conduct and thoughts of men, spends nearly his whole life in the fields, the mountains, or the small country villages of Judea; and in the very closing scenes of his life, will not so much as sleep within the walls of Jerusalem, but rests at the little village of Bethphage, walking in the morning, and returning in the evening, through the peaceful avenues of the mount of Olives, to and from his work of teaching in the temple.

It would thus naturally follow, both from the general tone and teaching of the Scriptures, and from the example of our Lord himself, that wherever Christianity was preached and accepted, there would be an immediate interest awakened in the works of God, as seen in the natural world.

The whole force of education, until very lately, has been directed in every possible way to the destruction of the love of nature. The only knowledge which has been considered essential among us is that of words, and, next after it, of the abstract sciences; while every liking shown by children for simple natural history has been either violently checked (if it took an inconvenient form for the housemaids), or else scrupulously limited to hours of play: so that it has really been impossible for any child earnestly to

study the works of God but against its con
science; and the love of nature has become inherently the characteristic of truants and idlers.
While also the art of drawing, which is of more
real importance to the human race than that of
writing (because people can hardly draw anything without being of some use both to themselves and others, and can hardly write anything
without wasting their own time and that of
others),—this art of drawing, I say, which
on plain and stern system should be taught to
every child, just as writing is,—has been so
neglected and abused, that there is not one man
in a thousand, even of its professed teachers,
who knows its first principles: and thus it needs
much ill-fortune or obstinacy—much neglect on
the part of his teachers, or rebellion on his own
—before a boy can get leave to use his eyes or
his fingers; so that those who *can* use them are
for the most part neglected or rebellious lads—
runaways and bad scholars—passionate, erratic,
self-willed, and restive against all forms of education; while your well-behaved and amiable
scholars are disciplined into blindness and palsy
of half their faculties.   Wherein there is at
once a notable ground for what difference we
have observed between the lovers of nature and
its despisers; between the somewhat immoral
and unrespectable watchfulness of the one

and the moral and respectable blindness of the other.

One more argument remains, and that, I believe, an unanswerable one. As, by the accident of education, the love of nature has been, among us, associated with *wilfulness*, so, by the accident of time, it has been associated with *faithlessness*. I traced, above, the peculiar mode in which this faithlessness was indicated ; but I never intended to imply, therefore, that it was an invariable concomitant of the love. Because it happens that, by various concurrent operations of evil, we have been led, according to those words of the Greek poet already quoted, " to dethrone the gods, and crown the whirlwind," it is no reason that we should forget there was once a time when " the Lord answered Job *out of* the whirlwind." And if we now take final and full view of the matter, we shall find that the love of nature, wherever it has existed, has been a faithful and sacred element of human feeling ; that is to say, supposing all circumstances otherwise the same with respect to two individuals, the one who loves nature most will be *always* found to have more *faith in God* than the other. It is intensely difficult, owing to the confusing and counter influences which always mingle in the data of the problem, to make this abstraction fairly ; but so far as we can do it, so far, I boldly assert, the result is constantly the same : the nature-worship will be found to bring with it such a sense of the presence and power of a Great Spirit as no mere reasoning can either induce or controvert ; and where that nature-worship is innocently pursued,—i.e. with due respect to other claims on time, feeling, and exertion, and associated with the higher principles of religion,—it becomes the channel of certain sacred truths, which by no other means can be conveyed.

This is not a statement which any investigation is needed to prove. It comes to us at once from the highest of all authority. The greater number of the words which are recorded in Scripture, as directly spoken to men by the lips of the Deity, are either simple revelations of His law, or special threatenings, commands, and promises relating to special events. But two passages of God's speaking, one in the Old and one in the New Testament, possess, it seems to me, a different character from any of the rest, having been uttered, the one to effect the last necessary change in the mind of a man whose piety was in other respects perfect ; and the other, as the first statement to all men of the principles of Christianity by Christ himself—I mean the 38th to 41st chapters of the book of Job, and the Sermon on the Mount. Now,

the first of these passages is, from beginning to
end, nothing else than a direction of the mind
which was to be perfected to humble observance
of the works of God in nature. And the other
consists only in the inculcation of *three* things :
1st, right conduct ; 2nd, looking for eternal life;
3rd, trusting God, through watchfulness of His
dealings with His creation : and the entire contents of the book of Job, and of the Sermon on
the Mount, will be found resolvable simply into
these three requirements from all men,—that
they should act rightly, hope for heaven, and
watch God's wonders and work in the earth ;
the right conduct being always summed up under
the three heads of *justice*, *mercy*, and *truth*, and
no mention of any doctrinal point whatsoever
occurring in either piece of divine teaching.

As far as I can judge of the ways of men, it
seems to me that the simplest and most necessary truths are always the last believed ; and I
suppose that well-meaning people in general
would rather regulate their conduct and creed
by almost any other portion of Scripture whatsoever, than by that Sermon on the Mount which
contains the things that Christ thought it first
necessary for all men to understand. Nevertheless, I believe the time will soon come for the
full force of these two passages of Scripture to
be accepted. Instead of supposing the love of

nature necessarily connected with the faithlessness of the age, I believe it is connected properly with the benevolence and liberty of the
age ; that it is precisely the most healthy element which distinctively belongs to us ; and
that out of it, cultivated no longer in levity or
ignorance, but in earnestness and as a duty, results will spring of an importance at present inconceivable ; and lights arise, which, for the
first time in man's history, will reveal to him the
true nature of his life, the true field for his
energies, and the true relations between him and
his Maker.

I will not endeavor here to trace the various
modes in which these results are likely to be effected, for this would involve an essay on education, on the uses of natural history, and the
probable future destiny of nations.   Somewhat
on these subjects I have spoken in other places;
and I hope to find time, and proper place, to say
more.   But one or two observations may be
made merely to suggest the directions in which
the reader may follow out the subject for himself.

The great mechanical impulses of the age, of
which most of us are so proud, are a mere passing fever, half-speculative, half-childish.   People
will discover at last that royal roads to anything
can no more be laid in iron than they can in

dust ; that there are, in fact, no royal roads to anywhere worth going to ; that if there were, it would that instant cease to be worth going to, —I mean so far as the things to be obtained are in any way estimable in terms of *price*. For there are two classes of precious things in the world : those that God gives us for nothing— sun, air, and life (both mortal life and immortal); and the secondarily precious things which he gives us for a price : these secondarily precious things, worldly wine and milk, can only be bought for definite money ; they never can be cheapened. No cheating nor bargaining will ever get a single thing out of nature's "establishment" at half-price. Do we want to be strong ?—we must work. To be hungry ?—we must starve. To be happy ?—we must be kind. To be wise ?—we must look and think. No changing of place at a hundred miles an hour, nor making of stuffs a thousand yards a minute, will make us one whit stronger, happier, or wiser. There was always more in the world than men could see, walked they ever so slowly; they will see it no better for going fast. And they will at last, and soon too, find out that their grand inventions for conquering (as they think) space and time, do, in reality, conquer nothing ; for space and time are, in their own essence, unconquerable, and besides did not

want any sort of conquering ; they wanted *using*.
A fool always wants to shorten space and time :
a wise man wants to lengthen both. A fool
wants to kill space and kill time : a wise man,
first to gain them, then to animate them. Your
railroad, when you come to understand it, is
only a device for making the world smaller:
and as for being able to talk from place to place,
that is, indeed, well and convenient ; but suppose you have, originally, nothing to say.*   We
shall be obliged at last to confess, what we
should long ago have known, that the really
precious things are thought and sight, not pace.
It does a bullet no good to go fast ; and a man,
no harm to go slow ; for his glory is not at all
in going, but in being.

 " Well ; but railroads and telegraphs are so
useful for communicating knowledge to savage
nations."   Yes, if you have any to give them.
If you know nothing *but* railroads, and can communicate nothing but aqueous vapor and gunpowder—what then ?   But if you have any other
thing than these to give, then the railroad is of
use only because it communicates that other
thing; and the question is—what that other
thing may be. Is it religion ? I believe if we
had really wanted to communicate that, we

---

 * " The light-outspeeding telegraph
  Bears nothing on its beam. " EMERSON.

could have done it in less than 1800 years, without steam. Most of the good religious communication that I remember has been done on
foot; and it cannot be easily done faster than
at foot pace. Is it science? But what science
—of motion, meat, and medicine? Well; when
you have moved your savage, and dressed your
savage, fed him with white bread, and shown
him how to set a limb,—what next? Follow
out that question. Suppose every obstacle
overcome; give your savage every advantage of
civilization to the full; suppose that you have
put the Red Indian in tight shoes; taught the
Chinese how to make Wedgwood's ware, and to
paint it with colors that will rub off; and persuaded all Hindoo women that it is more pious
to torment their husbands into graves than to
burn themselves at the burial,—what next?
Gradually, thinking on from point to point, we
shall come to perceive that all true happiness
and nobleness are near us, and yet neglected by
us; and that till we have learned how to be
happy and noble, we have not much to tell, even
to Red Indians. The delights of horse-racing
and hunting, of assemblies in the night instead
of the day, of costly and wearisome music, of
costly and burdensome dress, of chagrined con-
tention for place or power, or wealth, or the
eyes of the multitude; and all the endless occu-

pation without purpose, and idleness without rest, of our vulgar world, are not, it seems to me, enjoyments we need be ambitious to communicate. And all real and wholesome enjoyments possible to man have been just as possible to him, since first he was made of the earth, as they are now; and they are possible to him chiefly in peace. To watch the corn grow, and the blossoms set; to draw hard breath over ploughshare or spade; to read, to think, to love, to hope, to pray,—these are the things that make men happy; they have always had the power of doing these, they never *will* have power to do more. The world's prosperity or adversity depends upon our knowing and teaching these few things: but upon iron, or glass, or electricity, or steam, in no wise.

And I am Utopian and enthusiastic enough to believe, that the time will come when the world will discover this. It has now made its experiments in every possible direction but the right one; and it seems that it must, at last, try the right one, in a mathematical necessity. It has tried fighting, and preaching, and fasting, buying and selling, pomp and parsimony, pride and humiliation,—every possible manner of existence in which it could conjecture there was any happiness or dignity; and all the while, as it bought, sold, and fought, and fasted, and

wearied itself with policies, and ambitions, and
self-denials, God had placed its real happiness
in the keeping of the little mosses of the wayside, and of the clouds of the firmament. Now
and then a weary king, or a tormented slave,
found out where the true kingdoms of the world
were, and possessed himself, in a furrow or two
of garden ground, of a truly infinite dominion.
But the world would not believe their report,
and went on tramping down the mosses, and
forgetting the clouds, and seeking happiness in
its own way, until, at last, blundering and late,
came natural science; and in natural science
not only the observation of things, but the finding out of new uses for them. Of course the
world, having a choice left to it, went wrong as
usual, and thought that these mere material uses
were to be the sources of its happiness. It got
the clouds packed into iron cylinders, and made
it carry its wise self at their own cloud pace. It
got weavable fibres out of the mosses, and made
clothes for itself, cheap and fine,—here was
happiness at last. To go as fast as the clouds,
and manufacture everything out of anything,—
here was paradise indeed !

And now, when, in a little while, it is unpara-
dised again, if there were any other mistake that
the world could make, it would of course make
it. But I see not that there is any other; and,

standing fairly at its wits' end, having found
that going fast, when it is used to it, is no more
paradisiacal than going slow; and that all the
prints and cottons in Manchester cannot make
it comfortable in its mind, I do verily believe it
will come, finally, to understand that God paints
the clouds and shapes the moss-fibres, that men
may be happy in seeing him at his work, and
that in resting quietly beside him, and watching
his working, and—according to the power he
has communicated to ourselves, and the guidance he grants,—in carrying out his purposes
of peace and charity among all his creatures,
are the only real happinesses that ever were, or
will be, possible to mankind.

How far art is capable of helping us in such
happiness we hardly yet know; but I hope to be
able, in the subsequent parts of this work, to
give some data for arriving at a conclusion in
the matter. Enough has been advanced to re-
lieve the reader from any lurking suspicion of
unworthiness in our subject, and to induce him
to take interest in the mind and work of the
great painter who has headed the landscape
school among us. What further considerations
may, within any reasonable limits, be put before him, respecting the effect of natural scenery
on the human heart, I will introduce in their
proper places either as we examine, under Tur-

ner's guidance, the different classes of scenery
or at the close of the whole work; and therefore
I have only one point more to notice here,
namely, the exact relation between landscape
painting and natural science, properly so called.

For it may be thought that I have rashly assumed that the Scriptural authorities above
quoted apply to that partly superficial view of
nature which is taken by the landscape-painter
instead of to the accurate view taken by the
man of science. So far from there being rash-
ness in such an assumption, the whole language,
both of the book of Job and the Sermon on the
Mount, gives precisely the view of nature which
is taken by the uninvestigating affection of a
humble, but powerful mind. There is no dis-
section of muscles or counting of elements, but
the boldest and broadest glance at the apparent
facts, and the most magnificent metaphor in
expressing them. "His eyes are like the eyelids
of the morning. In his neck remaineth strength,
and sorrow is turned into joy before him." And
in the often repeated, never obeyed, command,
"Consider the lilies of the field," observe there
is precisely the delicate attribution of life which
we have seen to be the characteristic of the
modern view of landscape,—"They toil not."
There is no science, or hint of science; no
counting of petals, nor display of provisions for

sustenance: nothing but the expression of sympathy, at once the most childish, and the most profound,—" They toil not."

And we see in this, therefore, that the instinct which leads us thus to attribute life to the lowest forms of organic nature, does not necessarily spring from faithlessness, nor the deducing a moral out of them from an irregular and languid conscientiousness. In this, as in almost all things connected with moral discipline, the same results may follow from contrary causes; and as there are a good and evil contentment, a good and evil discontent, a good and evil care, fear, ambition, and so on, there are also good and evil forms of this sympathy with nature, and disposition to moralize over it. In general, active men, of strong sense and stern principle, do not care to see anything in a leaf, but vegetable tissue, and are so well convinced of useful moral truth, that it does not strike them as a new or notable thing when they find it in any way symbolized by material nature; hence there is a strong presumption, when first we perceive a tendency in any one to regard trees as living, and enunciate moral aphorisms over every pebble they stumble against, that such tendency proceeds from a morbid temperament, like Shelley's, or an inconstant one, like Jaques's. But when the active life is nobly ful-

filled, and the mind is then raised beyond it into
clear and calm beholding of the world around
us, the same tendency again manifests itself in
the most sacred way: the simplest forms of nature are strangely animated by the sense of the
Divine presence; the trees and flowers seem all,
in a sort, children of God; and we ourselves,
their fellows, made out of the same dust, and
greater than they only in having a greater portion of the Divine power exerted on our frame,
and all the common uses and palpably visible forms of things, become subordinate in our
minds to their inner glory,—to the mysterious
voices in which they talk to us about God, and
the changeful and typical aspects by which they
witness to us of holy truth, and fill us with obe-
dient, joyful, and thankful emotion.

It is in raising us from the first state of inactive
reverie to the second of useful thought, that
scientific pursuits are to be chiefly praised. But
in restraining us at this second stage, and checking the impulses towards higher contemplation,
they are to be feared or blamed. They may in
certain minds be consistent with such contemplation ; but only by an effort: in their nature
they are always adverse to it, having a tendency
to chill and subdue the feelings, and to resolve
all things into atoms and numbers. For most
men, an ignorant enjoyment is better than an

informed one; it is better to conceive the sky as a blue dome than a dark cavity, and the cloud as a golden throne than a sleety mist. I much question whether any one who knows optics, however religious he may be, can feel in equal degree the pleasure or reverence which an unlettered peasant may feel at the sight of a rainbow. And it is mercifully thus ordained, since the law of life, for a finite being, with respect to the works of an infinite one, must be always an infinite ignorance. We cannot fathom the mystery of a single flower, nor is it intended that we should; but that the pursuit of science should constantly be stayed by the love of beauty, and accuracy of knowledge by tenderness of emotion.

Nor is it even just to speak of the love of beauty as in all respects unscientific; for there is a science of the aspects of things as well as of their nature; and it is as much a fact to be noted in their constitution, that they produce such and such an effect upon the eye or heart (as, for instance, that minor scales of sound cause melancholy), as that they are made up of certain atoms or vibrations of matter.

We are too much in the habit of looking at falsehood in its darkest associations, and through the color of its worst purposes. That indignation which we profess to feel at deceit absolute, is indeed only at deceit malicious. We resent calumny, hypocrisy, and treachery, because they harm us, not because they are untrue. Take the detraction and the mischief from the untruth, and we are little offended by it; turn it into praise, and we may be pleased with it. And yet it is not calumny nor treachery that does the most harm in the world; they are continually crushed, and are felt only in being conquered. But it is the glistening and softly spoken lie; the amiable fallacy; the patriotic lie of the historian, the provident lie of the politician, the zealous lie of the partizan, the merciful lie of the friend, and the careless lie of each man to himself, that cast that black mystery over humanity, through which any man who pierces, we thank as we would thank any one who dug a well in a desert; happy in that the thirst for truth still remains with us, even when we have wilfully left the fountains of it.

It would be well if moralists less frequently confused the greatness of a sin with its unpardonableness. The two characters are altogether distinct. The greatness of a fault depends partly on the nature of the person against whom it is committed, partly upon the extent of its consequences. Its pardonableness depends, *humanly speaking*, on the degree of temptation to it. One class of circumstances determines the weight of

the attaching punishment, the other, the claim
to the remission of punishment ; and since it is
not easy for men to estimate the relative weight,
nor possible for them to know the relative consequences of crime, it is usually wise in them to
quit the care of such wise adjustments, and to
look on the other and clearer condition of cul-
pability, esteeming those faults greatest which
are committed under least temptation. I do not
mean to diminish the blame of the injurious and
malicious sin, of the selfish and deliberate falsity ;
yet it seems to me that the shortest way to check
the darker forms of deceit is to set more scrupu-
lous watch against those which have mingled,
unregarded and unchastised, with the current of
our life. Do not let us lie at all. Do not think
of one falsity as harmless, and another as slight,
and another as unintended. Cast them all aside ;
they may be light and accidental, but they are
an ugly soot from the smoke of the pit, for all
that ; and it is better that our hearts should be
kept clear of them, without over-care as to
which is the largest or blackest. Speaking truth
is like writing fair, and comes only by practice ;
it is less a matter of will than of habit ; and I
doubt if any occasion can be trivial which permits the practice and formation of such a habit.
To speak and act truth with constancy and precision is nearly as difficult, and perhaps as meri-

torious, as to speak it under intimidation or penalty; and it is a strange thought how many men there are, as I trust, who would hold it at the cost of fortune or life, for one who could hold it at the cost of a little daily trouble.

And seeing that of all sin there is, perhaps, no one more flatly opposite to the Almighty, no one more " wanting the good of virtue and of being," than this of lying, it is surely a strange insolence to fall into the foulness of it on light or no temptation, and surely becoming an honorable man to resolve that, whatever fallacies the necessary course of his life may compel him to bear or to believe, none shall disturb the serenity of his voluntary actions, nor diminish the reality of his chosen delights.

On the whole, these are much *sadder* ages than the early ones; not sadder in a noble and deep way, but in a dim, wearied way,—the way of ennui, and jaded intellect, and uncomfortableness of soul and body. The Middle Ages had their wars and agonies, but also intense delights. Their gold was dashed with blood; but ours is sprinkled with dust. Their life was interwoven with white and purple; ours is one seamless stuff of brown. Not that we are without apparent festivity, but festivity more or less forced, mistaken, embittered, incomplete—not of the heart.

How wonderfully, since Shakspeare's time, have we lost the power of laughing at bad jests! The very finish of our wit belies our gaiety.

The profoundest reason of this darkness of heart is, I believe, our want of faith. There never yet was a generation of men (savage or civilized) who, taken as a body, so wofully ful-filled the words, " having no hope, and without God in the world," as the present civilized Euro-pean race. A Red Indian or Otaheitan savage has more sense of a Divine existence round him, or government over him, than the plurality of refined Londoners and Parisians; and those among us who may in some sense be said to believe, are divided almost without exception into two broad classes, Romanist and Puritan; who but for the interfer-ence of the unbelieving portions of society, would, either of them, reduce the other sect as speedily as possible to ashes; the Romanist having always done so whenever he could, from the beginning of their separation, and the Puritan at this time holding himself in complacent expectation of the destruction of Rome by volcanic fire. Such division as this between persons nominally of one religion, that is to say, believing in the same God, and the same Revelation, cannot but be-come a stumbling-block of the gravest kind to all thoughtful and far-sighted men,—a stum-bling-block which they can only surmount under

the most favorable circumstances of early education. Hence, nearly all our powerful men in
this age of the world are unbelievers; the best of
them in doubt and misery; the worst in reckless
defiance; the plurality in plodding hesitation,
doing, as well as they can, what practical work
lies ready to their hands. Most of our scientific
men are in this last class; our popular authors
either set themselves definitely against all religious form, pleading for simply truth and benevolence (Thackeray, Dickens), or give themselves up to bitter and fruitless statement of facts
(De Balzac), or surface-painting (Scott), or careless blasphemy, sad or smiling (Byron, Béranger).
Our earnest poets, and deepest thinkers, are
doubtful and indignant (Tennyson, Carlyle);
one or two, anchored, indeed, but anxious, or
weeping (Wordsworth, Mrs. Browning); and of
these two, the first is not so sure of his anchor,
but that now and then it drags with him, even to
make him cry out,—

> "Great God, I had rather be
> A Pagan suckled in some creed outworn:
> So might I, standing on this pleasant lea,
> Have glimpses that would make me less forlorn."

The absence of care for personal beauty,
which is another great characteristic of the age,
adds to this feeling in a twofold way: first, by

turning all reverent thoughts away from human nature; and making us think of men as ridiculous or ugly creatures, getting through the world as well as they can, and spoiling it in doing so; not ruling it in a kingly way and crowning all its loveliness. In the Middle Ages hardly anything but vice could be caricatured, because virtue was always visibly and personally noble; now virtue itself is apt to inhabit such poor human bodies, that no aspect of it is invulnerable to jest; and for all fairness we have to seek to the flowers, for all sublimity, to the hills.

The same want of care operates, in another way, by lowering the standard of health, increasing the susceptibility to nervous or sentimental impressions, and thus adding to the other powers of nature over us whatever charm may be felt in her fostering the melancholy fancies of brooding idleness.

That is to everything created, pre-eminently useful, which enables it rightly and fully to perform the functions appointed to it by its Creator. Therefore, that we may determine what is chiefly useful to man, it is necessary first to determine the use of man himself.

Man's use and function is to be the witness of the glory of God, and to advance that glory by his reasonable obedience and resultant happiness.

Whatever enables us to fulfil this function, is in the pure and first sense of the word useful to us; pre-eminently, therefore, whatever sets the glory of God more brightly before us. But things that only help us to exist, are in a secondary and mean sense, useful, or rather, if they be looked for alone, they are useless and worse; for it would be better that we should not exist, than that we should guiltily disappoint the purposes of existence.

And yet people speak in this working age, when they speak from their hearts, as if houses, and lands, and food, and raiment were alone useful, and as if sight, thought, and admiration, were all profitless, so that men insolently call themselves Utilitarians, who would turn, if they had their way, themselves and their race into vegetables; men whothink, as far as such can be said to think, that the meat is more than the life, and the raiment than the body, who look to the earth as a stable, and to its fruit as fodder; vine-dressers and husbandmen, who love the corn they grind, and the grapes they crush, better than the gardens of the angels upon the slopes of Eden; hewers of wood and drawers of water, who think that the wood they hew and the water they draw, are better than the pine forests that cover the mountains like the shadow of God, and than the great rivers that move like eternity.

It seems to me that much of what is great, and to all men beneficial, has been wrought by those who neither intended nor knew the good they did, and that many mighty harmonies have been discoursed by instruments that had been dumb or discordant, but that God knew their stops. The Spirit of Prophecy consisted with the avarice of Balaam, and the disobedience of Saul. Could we spare from its page that parable, which he said, who saw the vision of the Almighty, falling into a trance, but having his eyes open, though we know that the sword of his punishment was then sharp in its sheath beneath him in the plains of Moab? or shall we not lament with David over the shield cast away on the Gilboa mountains, of him to whom God gave *another heart* that day, when he turned his back to go from Samuel? It is not our part to look hardly, nor to look always, to the character or the deeds of men, but to accept from all of them, and to hold fast that which we can prove good, and feel to be ordained for us.

It is not possible for a Christian man to walk across so much as a rood of the natural earth, with mind unagitated and rightly poised, without receiving strength and hope from some stone,

flower, leaf, or sound, nor without a sense of a
dew falling upon him out of the sky; though, I
say, this falsity is not wholly and in terms admitted, yet it seems to be partly and practically
so in much of the doing and teaching even of
holy men, who in the recommending of the love
of God to us, refer but seldom to those things
in which it is most abundantly and immediately
shown; though they insist much on his giving
of bread, and raiment, and health (which he
gives to all inferior creatures), they require us
not to thank him for that glory of his works
which he has permitted us alone to perceive:
they tell us often to meditate in the closet, but
they send us not, like Isaac, into the fields at
even; they dwell on the duty of self-denial, but
they exhibit not the duty or delight. Now there
are reasons for this, manifold in the toil and
warfare of an earnest mind, which, in its efforts
at the raising of men from utter loss and misery,
has often but little time or disposition to take
heed of anything more than the bare life, and
of those so occupied it is not for us to judge;
but I think, that, of the weaknesses, distresses,
vanities, schisms, and sins, which often even in
the holiest men, diminish their usefulness, and
mar their happiness, there would be fewer, if in
their struggle with nature fallen, they sought
for more aid from nature undestroyed. It seems

to me that the real sources of bluntness in the
feelings towards the splendor of the grass and
glory of the flower, are less to be found in ardor
of occupation, in seriousness of compassion, or
heavenliness of desire, than in the turning of the
eye at intervals of rest too selfishly within; the
want of power to shake off the anxieties of actual and near interest, and to leave results in
God's hands; the scorn of all that does not
seem immediately apt for our purposes or open
to our understanding, and perhaps something of
pride, which desires rather to investigate than
to feel. I believe that the root of almost every
schism and heresy from which the Christian
church has ever suffered, has been the effort of
men to earn, rather than to receive, their salva-
tion.

Deep though the causes of thankfulness
must be to every people at peace with others
and at unity with itself, there are causes of fear
also, a fear greater than of sword and sedition;
that dependence on God may be forgotten because the bread is given and the water is sure;
that gratitude to him may cease because his
constancy of protection has taken the semblance
of a natural law; that heavenly hope may grow
faint amid the full fruition of the world; that
selfishness may take place of undemanded devotion, compassion be lost in vain-glory, and love

in dissimulation; that enervation may succeed to strength, apathy to patience, and noise of jesting words and foulness of dark thoughts to the earnest purity of the girded loins and the burning lamp. About the river of human life there is a wintry wind, though a heavenly sunshine; the iris colors its agitation; the frost fixes upon its repose! Let us beware that our rest become not the rest of stones, which so long as they are torrent-tossed and thunder-stricken, maintain their majesty, but when the stream is silent, and the storm passed, suffer the grass to cover them and the lichen to feed on them, and are ploughed down into dust.

There is no action so slight, nor so mean, but it may be done to a great purpose, and ennobled therefore; nor is any purpose so great but that slight actions may help it, and may be so done as to help it much, most especially that chief of all purposes, the pleasing of God. Hence George Herbert

> " A servant with this clause
>   Makes drudgery divine;
> Who sweeps a room, as for thy laws,
>   Makes that and the action fine."

We treat God with irreverence by banishing him from our thoughts, not by referring to his

will on slight occasions. His is not the finite
authority or intelligence which cannot be troubled with small things. There is nothing so small
but that we may honor God by asking his guidance of it, or insult him by taking it into our
own hands; and what is true of the Deity is
equally true of his Revelation. We use it most
reverently when most habitually; our insolence
is in ever acting without reference to it; our true
honoring of it is in its universal application.

There is not any part of our feeling or nature,
nor can there be through eternity, which shall
not be in some way influenced and affected by
the fall, and that not in any way of degradation,
for the renewing in the divinity of Christ is a
nobler condition than ever that of Paradise, and
yet throughout eternity it must imply and refer
to the disobedience, and the corrupt state of sin
and death, and the suffering of Christ himself,
which can we conceive of any redeemed soul as
for an instant forgetting, or as remembering
without sorrow? Neither are the alternations of
joy and such sorrow as by us is inconceivable,
being only as it were a softness and silence in
the pulse of an infinite felicity, inconsistent with
the state even of the unfallen, for the angels
who rejoice over repentance cannot but feel an
uncomprehended pain as they try and try again

in vain whether they may not warm hard hearts
with the brooding of their kind wings.

God appoints to every one of his creatures a
separate mission, and if they discharge it honor-
ably, if they quit themselves like men, and faithfully follow that light which is in them, withdrawing from it all cold and quenchless influence,
there will assuredly come of it such burning as,
according to its appointed mode and measure,
shall shine before men, and be of service constant and holy. Degrees infinite of lustre there
must always be, but the weakest among us has a
gift, however seemingly trivial, which is peculiar
to him, and which, worthily used, will be a gift
also to his race for ever—" Fool not," says
George Herbert,

> " For all may have,
> If they dare choose, a glorious life or grave."

Let us not forget, that if honor be for the
dead, gratitude can only be for the living. He
who has once stood beside the grave, to look
back upon the companionship which has been
for ever closed, feeling how impotent *there* are
the wild love, or the keen sorrow, to give one instant's pleasure to the pulseless heart, or atone
in the lowest measure to the departed spirit for
the hour of unkindness, will scarcely, for the

future, incur that debt to the heart, which can only be discharged to the dust. But the lesson which men receive as individuals, they do not learn as nations. Again and again they have seen their noblest descend into the grave, and have thought it enough to garland the tomb-stone when they had not crowned the brow, and to pay the honor to the ashes, which they had denied to the spirit. Let it not displease them that they are bidden, amid the tumult and the dazzle of their busy life, to listen to the few voices, and watch for the few lamps, which God has toned and lighted to charm and to guide them, that they may not learn their sweetness by their silence, nor their light by their decay.

Aristotle has subtly noted that " we call not men intemperate so much with respect to the scents of roses or herb-perfumes as of ointments and of condiments." For the fact is, that of scents artificially prepared the extreme desire is intemperance, but of natural and God-given scents, which take their part in the harmony and pleasantness of creation, there can hardly be in-temperance; not that there is any absolute dif-ference between the two kinds, but that these are likely to be received with gratitude and joy-fulness rather than those, so that we despise the seeking of essences and unguents, but not the sowing of violets along our garden banks. But all things may be elevated by affection, as the spikenard of Mary, and in the Song of Solomon, the myrrh upon the handles of the lock, and that of Isaac concerning his son. And the general law for all these pleasures is, that when sought in the abstract and ardently, they are foul things, but when received with thankfulness and with reference to God's glory, they become theoretic (the exulting, reverent, and grateful perception of pleasantness, I call *theoria*); and so I can find something divine in the sweetness of wild fruits, as well as in the pleasantness of the pure air, and the tenderness of its natural perfumes that come and go as they list.

The pleasures of sight and hearing are given as *gifts*. They answer not any purposes of mere existence, for the distinction of all that is useful or dangerous to us might be made, and often is made, by the eye, without its receiving the slightest pleasure of sight. We might have learned to distinguish fruits and grain from flowers, without having any superior pleasure in the aspect of the latter. And the ear might have learned to distinguish the sounds that communicate ideas, or to recognize intimations of elemental danger, without perceiving either music in the voice, or majesty in the thunder. And as these pleasures have no function to perform. so there is no limit to their continuance in the accomplishment of their end, for *they are an end in themselves*, and so may be perpetual with all of us—being in no way destructive, but rather increasing in exquisiteness by repetition.

In whatever is an object of life, in whatever may be infinitely and for itself desired, we may be sure there is something of divine, for God will not make anything an object of life to his creatures which does not point to, or partake of, himself.

I believe one of the worst symptoms of modern society to be, its notion of great inferiority, and ungentlemanliness, as necessarily belonging to the character of a tradesman. I believe tradesmen may be, ought to be—often are, more gentlemen than idle and useless people: and I believe that art may do noble work by recording in the hall of each trade, the services which men belonging to that trade have done for their country, both preserving the portraits, and recording the important incidents in the lives, of those who have made great advances in commerce and civilization. We are stewards or ministers of whatever talents are entrusted to us. Is it not a strange thing, that while we more or less accept the meaning of that saying, so long as it is considered metaphorical, we never accept its meaning in its own terms? You know the lesson is given us under the form of a story about money. Money was given to the servants to make use of: the unprofitable servant dug in the earth, and hid his Lord's money. Well, we, in our poetical and spiritual application of this, say, that of course money doesn't mean money, it means wit, it means intellect, it means influence in high quarters, it means everything in the world except itself. And do not you see what a pretty and pleasant come-off there is for most of us, in this spiritual application? Of course, if we had wit, we would use it for the good of our fellow-creatures. But we haven't wit. Of course, if we had influence with the bishops, we would use it for the good of the Church; but we haven't any influence with the bishops. Of course, if we had political power, we would use it for the good of the nation; but we have no political power; we have no talents entrusted to *us* of any sort or kind. It is true we have a little money, but the parable can't possibly mean anything so vulgar as money; our money's our own.

I believe, if you think seriously of this matter, you will feel that the first and most literal application is just as necessary a one as any other —that the story does very specially mean what it says—plain money; and that the reason we

don't at once believe it does so, is a sort of tacit
idea that while thought, wit, and intellect, and
all power of birth and position, are indeed *given*
to us, and, therefore, to be laid out for the Giver,
—our wealth has not been given to us; but we
have worked for it, and have a right to spend it
as we choose. I think you will find that is the
real substance of our understanding in this matter. Beauty, we say, is given by God—it is a
talent; strength is given by God—it is a talent;
position is given by God—it is a talent; but
money is proper wages for our day's work—it is
not a talent, it is a due. We may justly spend
it on ourselves, if we have worked for it.

And there would be some shadow of excuse
for this, were it not that the very power of making the money is itself only one of the applica-
tions of that intellect or strength which we confess to be talents. Why is one man richer than
another? Because he is more industrious,
more persevering, and more sagacious. Well,
who made him more persevering and more
sagacious than others? That power of en-
durance, that quickness of apprehension, that
calmness of judgment, which enable him to
seize the opportunities that others lose, and per-
sist in the lines of conduct in which others fail
—are these not talent?—are they not in the
present state of the world among the most dis-

tinguished and influential of mental gifts? And is it not wonderful, that while we should be utterly ashamed to use a superiority of body, in order to thrust our weaker companions aside from some place of advantage, we unhesitatingly use our superiorities of mind to thrust them back from whatever good that strength of mind can attain. You would be indignant if you saw a strong man walk into a theatre or a lecture-room, and calmly choosing the best place, take his feeble neighbor by the shoulder, and turn him out of it into the back seats, or the street. You would be equally indignant if you saw a stout fellow thrust himself up to a table where some hungry children were being fed, and reach his arm over their heads and take their bread from them. But you are not the least indignant if when a man has stoutness of thought and swiftness of capacity, and, instead of being long-armed only, has the much greater gift of being long-headed—you think it perfectly just that he should use his intellect to take the bread out of the mouths of all the other men in the town who are of the same trade with him; or use his breadth and sweep of sight to gather some branch of the commerce of the country into one great cobweb, of which he is himself to be the central spider, making every thread vibrate with the points of his claws, and com-

manding every avenue with the facets of his
eyes. You see no injustice in this.

But there is injustice; and, let us trust, one of
which honorable men will at no very distant
period disdain to be guilty. In some degree,
however, it is indeed not unjust; in some degree
it is necessary and intended. It is assuredly
just that idleness should be surpassed by energy;
that the widest influence should be possessed by
those who are best able to wield it; and that a
wise man, at the end of his career, should be
better off than a fool. But for that reason, is
the fool to be wretched, utterly crushed down,
and left in all the suffering which his conduct
and capacity naturally inflict?—Not so. What
do you suppose fools were made for? That
you might tread upon them, and starve them,
and get the better of them in every possible
way? By no means. They were made that
wise people might take care of them. That is
the true and plain fact concerning the relations
of every strong and wise man to the world
about him. He has his strength given him, not
that he may crush the weak, but that he may
support and guide them. In his own household
he is to be the guide and the support of his
children; out of his household he is still to be
the father, that is, the guide and support of the
weak and the poor; not merely of the meritori-

ously weak and the innocently poor, but of the guiltily and punishably poor; of the men who ought to have known better—of the poor who ought to be ashamed of themselves. It is nothing to give pension and cottage to the widow who has lost her son; it is nothing to give food and medicine to the workman who has broken his arm, or the decrepit woman wasting in sickness. But it is something to use your time and strength to war with the waywardness and thoughtlessness of mankind; to keep the erring workman in your service till you have made him an unerring one; and to direct your fellow-merchant to the opportunity which his dulness would have lost. This is much; but it is yet more, when you have fully achieved the superiority which is due to you, and acquired the wealth which is the fitting reward of your sagacity, if you solemnly accept the responsibility of it, as it is the helm and guide of labor far and near. For you who have it in your hands, are in reality the pilots of the power and effort of the State. It is entrusted to you as an authority to be used for good or evil, just as completely as kingly authority was ever given to a prince, or military command to a captain. And, according to the quantity of it that you have in your hands, you are the arbiters of the will and work of England; and the whole issue, whether

the work of the State shall suffice for the State
or not, depends upon you. You may stretch
out your sceptre over the heads of the English
laborers, and say to them, as they stoop to its
waving, " Subdue this obstacle that has baffled
our fathers, put away this plague that consumes
our children; water these dry places, plough
these desert ones, carry this food to those who
are in hunger; carry this light to those who are
in darkness; carry this life to those who are in
death;" or on the other side you may say to her
laborers: " Here am I; this power is in my hand;
come, build a mound here for me to be throned
upon, high and wide; come, make crowns for
my head, that men may see them shine from far
away; come, weave tapestries for my feet, that
I may tread softly on the silk and purple; come,
dance before me, that I may be gay; and sing
sweetly to me, that I may slumber; so shall I
live in joy and die in honor." And better than
such an honorable death, it were that the day
had perished wherein we were born, and the
night in which it was said there is a child conceived.

I trust that in a little while, there will be few
of our rich men who, through carelessness or
covetousness, thus forfeit the glorious office
which is intended for their hands. I said, just
now, that wealth ill-used was as the net of the

spider, entangling and destroying: but wealth
well used, is as the net of the sacred fisher who
gathers souls of men out of the deep. A time
will come—I do not think even now it is far
from us—when this golden net of the world's
wealth will be spread abroad as the flaming
meshes of morning cloud are over the sky;
bearing with them the joy of light and the dew
of the morning, as well as the summons to honorable and peaceful toil. What less can we
hope from your wealth than this, rich men of
England, when once you feel fully how, by the
strength of your possessions—not, observe, by
the exhaustion, but by the administration of
them and the power—you can direct the acts,—
command the energies—inform the ignorance,—
prolong the existence, of the whole human race;
and how, even of worldly wisdom, which man
employs faithfully, it is true, not only that her
ways are pleasantness, but that her paths are
peace; and that, for all the children of men, as
well as for those to whom she is given, Length
of days are in her right hand, as in her left hand
Riches and Honor?

We are too much in the habit of considering
happy accidents as what are called "special
Providences;" and thinking that when any great
work needs to be done. the man who is to do it

will certainly be pointed out by Providence, be he shepherd or sea-boy; and prepared for his work by all kinds of minor providences, in the best possible way. Whereas all the analogies of God's operations in other matters prove the contrary of this; we find that "of thousand seeds, he often brings but one to bear," often not one; and the one seed which he appoints to bear is allowed to bear crude or perfect fruit according to the dealings of the husbandman with it. And there cannot be a doubt in the mind of any person accustomed to take broad and logical views of the world's history, that its events are ruled by Providence in precisely the same manner as its harvests; that the seeds of good and evil are broadcast among men, just as the seeds of thistles and fruits are; and that according to the force of our industry, and wisdom of our husbandry, the ground will bring forth to us figs or thistles. So that when it seems needed that a certain work should be done for the world, and no man is there to do it, we have no right to say that God did not wish it to be done, and therefore sent no man able to do it. The probability (if I wrote my own convictions, I should say certainty) is, that he sent many men, hundreds of men, able to do it; and that we have rejected them, or crushed them; by our previous folly of conduct or of institution, we have rendered it impossible to distinguish, or impossible to reach them; and when the need for them comes, and we suffer for the want of them, it is not that God refuses to send us deliverers, and specially appoints all our consequent sufferings; but that he has sent, and we have refused, the deliverers; and the pain is then wrought out by his eternal law, as surely as famine is wrought out by eternal law for a nation which will neither plough nor sow. No less are we in error in supposing, as we so frequently do, that if a man be found, he is sure to be in all respects fitted for the work to be done, as the key is to the lock; and that every accident which happened in the forging him, only adapted him more truly to the wards. It is pitiful to hear historians beguiling themselves and their readers, by tracing in the early history of great men, the minor circumstances which fitted them for the work they did, without ever taking notice of the other circumstances which as assuredly unfitted them for it; so concluding that miraculous interposition prepared them in all points for everything, and that they did all that could have been desired or hoped for from them: whereas the certainty of the matter is that, throughout their lives, they were thwarted and corrupted by some things as certainly as they were helped and disciplined by others; and that, in the kindliest and most reverent view which can justly be taken of them, they were but poor mistaken creatures, struggling with a world more profoundly mistaken than they;— assuredly sinned against, or sinning in thousands of ways, and bringing out at last a maimed result—not what they might or ought to have done, but all that could be done against the world's resistance, and in spite of their own sorrowful falsehood to themselves.

And this being so, it is the practical duty of a wise nation, first to withdraw, as far as may be, its youth from destructive influences;—then to try its material as far as possible, and to lose the use of none that is good. I do not mean by "withdrawing from destructive influences" the keeping of youths out of trials; but the keeping them out of the way of things purely and absolutely mischievous. I do not mean that we should shade our green corn in all heat, and shelter it in all frost, but only that we should dyke out the inundation from it, and drive the fowls away from it. Let your youth labor and suffer; but do not let it starve, nor steal, nor blaspheme.

Examine well the channels of your admiration, and you will find that they are, in verity, as unchangeable as the channels of your heart's blood; that just as by the pressure of a bandage, or by perpetual and unwholesome action of some part of the body, that blood may be wasted or arrested, and in its stagnancy cease to nourish the frame, or in its disturbed flow affect it with incurable disease, so also admiration itself may, by the bandages of fashion, bound close over the eyes and the arteries of the soul, be arrested in its natural pulse and healthy flow; but that whenever the artificial pressure is removed, it will return into that bed which has been traced for it by the finger of God.

Custom has no real influence upon our feelings of the beautiful, except in dulling and checking them. You see the broad blue sky every day over your heads; but you do not for that reason determine blue to be more or less beautiful than you did at first; you are unaccustomed to see stones as blue as the sapphire, but you do not for that reason think the sapphire less beautiful than other stones. The blue color is everlastingly appointed by the Deity to be a source of delight.

Let us think for a few moments what romance and Utopianism mean.

First, romance. In consequence of the many absurd fictions which long formed the elements of romance writing, the word romance is sometimes taken as synonymous with falsehood.

Thus the French talk of *Des Romans*, and thus the English use the word Romancing.

But in this sense we had much better use the word falsehood at once. It is far plainer and clearer. And if in this sense I put anything romantic before you, pray pay no attention to it, or to me.

In the second place. Because young people are particularly apt to indulge in reverie, and imaginative pleasures, and to neglect their plain and practical duties, the word *romantic* has come to signify weak, foolish, speculative, unpractical, unprincipled. In all these cases it would be much better to say weak, foolish, unpractical, unprincipled. The words are clearer. If in this sense, also, I put anything romantic before you, pray pay no attention to me.

The real and proper use of the word *romantic* is simply to characterise an improbable or unaccustomed degree of beauty, sublimity, or virtue. For instance, in matters of history, is not the Retreat of the Ten Thousand romantic? Is not the death of Leonidas? of the Horatii? On the other hand, you find nothing romantic, though much that is monstrous, in the excesses of Tiberius or Commodus. So again, the battle of Agincourt is romantic, and of Bannockburn, simply because there was an extraordinary display of human virtue in both those battles,

But there is no romance in the battles of the last Italian campaign, in which mere feebleness and distrust were on one side, mere physical force on the other. And even in fiction, the opponents of virtue, in order to be romantic, must have sublimity mingled with their vice. It is not the knave, not the ruffian, that are romantic, but the giant and the dragon; and these, not because they are false, but because they are majestic. So again as to beauty. You feel that armor is romantic because it is a beautiful dress, and you are not used to it. You do not feel there is anything romantic in the paint and shells of a Sandwich Islander, for these are not beautiful.

So then, observe, this feeling which you are accustomed to despise—this secret and poetical enthusiasm in all your hearts, which, as practical men, you try to restrain—is indeed one of the holiest parts of your being. It is the instinctive delight in, and admiration for, sublimity, beauty, and virtue, unusually manifested. And so far from being a dangerous guide, it is the truest part of your being. It is even truer than your consciences. A man's conscience may be utterly perverted and led astray; but so long as the feelings of romance endure within us, they are unerring—they are as true to what is right and lovely as the needle to the north; and all that you have to do is to add to the enthusiastic sentiment, the majestic judgment—to mingle prudence and foresight with imagination and admiration, and you have the perfect human soul. But the great evil of these days is that we try to destroy the romantic feeling, instead of bridling and directing it.   Mark what Young says of the men of the world:

> "They, who think nought so strong of the romance,
>   So rank knight-errant, as a real friend."

And they are right.   True friendship is romantic, to the men of the world—true affection is romantic—true religion is romantic; and if you were to ask me who of all powerful and popular writers in the cause of error had wrought most harm to their race, I should hesitate in reply whether to name Voltaire or Byron, or the last most ingenious and most venomous of the degraded philosophers of Germany, or rather Cervantes, for he cast scorn upon the holiest principles of humanity—he, of all men, most helped forward the terrible change in the soldiers of Europe, from the spirit of Bayard to the spirit of Bonaparte,* helped to change loyalty

---

* I mean no scandal against the *present* emperor of the French, whose truth has, I believe, been as conspicuous in the late political negotiations, as his decision and prudence have been throughout the whole course of his government.

into license, protection into plunder, truth into treachery, chivalry into selfishness; and since his time, the purest impulses and the noblest purposes have perhaps been oftener stayed by the devil, under the name of Quixotism, than under any other base name or false allegation.

Quixotism, or Utopianism: that is another of the devil's pet words. I believe the quiet admission which we are all of us so ready to make, that, because things have long been wrong, it is impossible they should ever be right, is one of the most fatal sources of misery and crime from which this world suffers. Whenever you hear a man dissuading you from attempting to do well, on the ground that perfection is "Utopian," beware of that man. Cast the word out of your dictionary altogether. There is no need for it. Things are either possible or impossible—you can easily determine which, in any given state of human science. If the thing is impossible, you need not trouble yourselves about it; if possible, try for it. It is very Utopian to hope for the entire doing away with drunkenness and misery out of the Canongate; but the Utopianism is not our business—the *work* is. It is Utopian to hope to give every child in this kingdom the knowledge of God from its youth; but the Utopianism is not our business—the *work* is.

You know how often it is difficult to be wisely

charitable, to do good without multiplying the
sources of evil. You know that to give alms is
nothing unless you give thought also; and that
therefore it is written, not "blessed is he that
feedeth the poor," but, "blessed is he that *consid-
ereth* the poor."   And you know that a little
thought and a little kindness are often worth
more than a great deal of money.

Now this charity of thought is not merely to be
exercised towards the poor; it is to be exercised
towards all men.   There is assuredly no action
of our social life, however unimportant, which,
by kindly thought, may not be made to have a
beneficial influence upon others; and it is impossible to spend the smallest sum of money,
for any not absolutely necessary purpose, without a grave responsibility attaching to the manner of spending it.   The object we ourselves
covet may, indeed, be desirable and harmless,
so far as we are concerned, but the providing us
with it may, perhaps, be a very prejudicial occupation to some one else.   And then it becomes
instantly a moral question, whether we are to
indulge ourselves or not.   Whatever we wish to
buy, we ought first to consider not only if the
thing be fit for us, but if the manufacture of it
be a wholesome and happy one; and if, on the
whole, the sum we are going to spend will do as
much good spent in this way as it would if spent

in any other way. It may be said that we have not time to consider all this before we make a purchase. But no time could be spent in a more important duty; and God never imposes a duty without giving the time to do it. Let us, however, only acknowledge the principle;—once make up your mind to allow the consideration of the *effect* of your purchases to regulate the *kind* of your purchase, and you will soon easily find grounds enough to decide upon. The plea of ignorance will never take away our responsibilities. It is written, " If thou sayest, Behold we knew it not; doth not he that pondereth the heart consider it ? and he that keepeth thy soul, doth not he know it ?"

There is another branch of decorative art in which I am sorry to say we cannot, at least under existing circumstances, indulge ourselves, with the hope of doing good to anybody, I mean the great and subtle art of dress.

And here I must interrupt the pursuit of our subject for a moment or two, in order to state one of the principles of political economy, which, though it is, I believe, now sufficiently understood and asserted by the leading masters of the science, is not yet, I grieve to say, acted upon by the plurality of those who have the management of riches. Whenever we spend money, we of course set people to work: that is the meaning

of spending money; we may, indeed, lose it
without employing anybody; but, whenever we
spend it, we set a number of people to work,
greater or less, of course, according to the rate
of wages, but in the long run, proportioned to
the sum we spend. Well, your shallow people,
because they see that however they spend money
they are always employing somebody, and, therefore, doing some good, think and say to themselves, that it is all one *how* they spend it—that
all their apparently selfish luxury is, in reality,
unselfish, and is doing just as much good as if
they gave all their money away, or perhaps more
good; and I have heard foolish people even
declare it is a principle of political economy,
that whoever invented a new want conferred a
good on the community. I have not words
strong enough—at least I could not, without
shocking you, use the words which would be
strong enough—to express my estimate of the
absurdity and the mischievousness of this popular fallacy. So putting a great restraint upon
myself, and using no hard words, I will simply
try to state the nature of it, and the extent of
its influence.

Granted, that whenever we spend money for
whatever purpose, we set people to work; and
passing by, for the moment, the question whether
the work we set them to is all equally healthy

and good for them, we will assume that whenever we spend a guinea we provide an equal
number of people with healthy maintenance for
a given time. But, by the way in which we
spend it, we entirely direct the labor of those
people during that given time. We become
their masters or mistresses, and we compel them
to produce, within a certain period, a certain
article. Now, that article may be a useful and
lasting one, or it may be a useless and perishable
one—it may be one useful to the whole community, or useful only to ourselves. And our selfishness and folly, or our virtue and prudence, are
shown, not by our spending money, but by our
spending it for the wrong or right thing; and we
are wise and kind, not in maintaining a certain
number of people for a given period, but only in
requiring them to produce, during that period,
the kind of things which shall be useful to
society, instead of those which are only useful to
ourselves.

Thus, for instance: if you are a young lady,
and employ a certain number of sempstresses for
a given time, in making a given number of simple
and serviceable dresses, suppose, seven; of which
you can wear one yourself for half the winter,
and give six away to poor girls who have none,
you are spending your money unselfishly. But
if you employ the same number of sempstresses

for the same number of days, in making four, or
five, or six beautiful flounces for your own ball-
dress—flounces which will clothe no one but
yourself, and which you will yourself be unable
to wear at more than one ball—you are employing your money selfishly.   You have maintained
indeed, in each case the same number of people;
but in the one case you have directed their labor
to the service of the community; in the other
case you have consumed it wholly upon yourself.   I don't say you are never to do so; I don't
say you ought not sometimes to think of yourselves only, and to make yourselves as pretty as
you can; only do not confuse coquettishness with
benevolence, nor cheat yourselves into thinking
that all the finery you can wear is so much put
into the hungry mouths of those beneath you: it
is not so; it is what you yourselves, whether you
will or no, must sometimes instinctively feel it to
be—it is what those who stand shivering in the
streets, forming a line to watch you as you step
out of your carriages, *know* it to be; those fine
dresses do not mean that so much has been put
into their mouths, but that so much has been
taken out of their mouths.   The real politico-
economical signification of every one of those
beautiful toilettes, is just this; that you have
had a certain number of people put for a certain
number of days wholly under your authority, by

the sternest of slave-masters,—hunger and cold; and you have said to them, "I will feed you, indeed, and clothe you, and give you fuel for so many days; but during those days you shall work for me only: your little brothers need clothes, but you shall make none for them; your sick friend needs clothes, but you shall make none for her; you yourself will soon need another, and a warmer dress; but you shall make none for yourself. You shall make nothing but lace and roses for me; for this fortnight to come, you shall work at the patterns and petals, and then I will crush and consume them away in an hour." You will perhaps answer—"It may not be particularly benevolent to do this, and we won't call it so; but at any rate we do no wrong in taking their labor when we pay them their wages: if we pay for their work we have a right to it." No;—a thousand times no. The labor which you have paid for, does indeed become, by the act of purchase, your own labor: you have bought the hands and the time of those workers; they are, by right and justice, your own hands, your own time. But have you a right to spend your own time, to work with your own hands, only for your own advantage?—much more, when, by purchase, you have invested your own person with the strength of others; and added to your own life, a part of the life of others? You may, indeed, to a certain extent, use their labor for your delight; remember, I am making no general assertions against splendor of dress, or pomp of accessaries of life; on the contrary, there are many reasons for thinking that we do not at present attach enough importance to beautiful dress, as one of the means of influencing general taste and character. But I *do* say, that you must weigh the value of what you ask these workers to produce for you in its own distinct balance; that on its own worthiness or desirableness rests the question of your kindness, and not merely on the fact of your having employed people in producing it: and I say farther, that as long as there are cold and nakedness in the land around you, so long there can be no question at all but that splendor of dress is a crime. In due time, when we have nothing better to set people to work at, it may be right to let them make lace and cut jewels; but, as long as there are any who have no blankets for their beds, and no rags for their bodies, so long it is blanket-making and tailoring we must set people to work at—not lace.

And it would be strange, if at any great assembly which, while it dazzled the young and the thoughtless, beguiled the gentler hearts that beat beneath the embroidery, with a placid sensation of luxurious benevolence—as if by all that they wore in waywardness of beauty, comfort had first been given to the distressed, and aid to the indigent; it would be strange, I say, if, for a moment, the spirits of Truth and of Terror, which walk invisibly among the masques of the earth, would lift the dimness from our erring thoughts, and show us how—inasmuch as the sums exhausted for that magnificence would have given back the failing breath to many an unsheltered outcast on moor and street—they who wear it have literally entered into partnership with Death; and dressed themselves in his spoils. Yes, if the veil could be lifted not only from your thoughts but from your human sight, you would see—the angels do see—on those gay white dresses of yours, strange dark spots, and crimson patterns that you knew not of—spots of the inextinguishable red that all the seas cannot wash away; yes, and among the pleasant flowers that crown your fair heads, and glow on your wreathed hair, you would see that one weed was always twisted which no one thought of—the grass that grows on graves.

It was not, however, this last, this clearest and most appalling view of our subject, that I intended to ask you to take this evening; only it is impossible to set any part of the matter in its true light, until we go to the root of it. But the point which it is our special business to con-

sider is, not whether costliness of dress is contrary to charity; but whether it is not contrary
to mere worldly wisdom: whether, even supposing we knew that splendor of dress did not cost
suffering or hunger, we might not put the splendor better in other things than dress.   And,
supposing our mode of dress were really graceful or beautiful, this might be a very doubtful
question; for I believe true nobleness of dress
to be an important means of education, as it
certainly is a necessity to any nation which
wishes to possess living art, concerned with portraiture of human nature.   No good historical
painting ever yet existed, or ever can exist,
where the dresses of the people of the time are
not beautiful: and had it not been for the lovely and fantastic dressing of the 13th to the 16th
centuries, neither French, nor Florentine, nor
Venetian art could have risen to anything like
the rank it reached.   Still, even then, the best
dressing was never the costliest; and its effect
depended much more on its beautiful, and, in
early times, modest, arrangement, and on the
simple and lovely masses of its color, than on
gorgeousness of clasp or embroidery.   Whether
we can ever return to any of those more perfect
types of form is questionable; but there can be
no question, that all the money we spend on the
forms of dress at present worn, is, so far as any

good purpose is concerned, wholly lost. Mind, in saying this, I reckon among good purposes the purpose which young ladies are said sometimes to entertain—of being married; but they would be married quite as soon (and probably to wiser and better husbands) by dressing quietly as by dressing brilliantly; and I believe it would only be needed to lay fairly and largely before them the real good which might be effected by the sums they spend in toilettes, to make them trust at once only to their bright eyes and braided hair for all the mischief they have a mind to. I wish we could, for once, get the statistics of a London season. There was much complaining talk in Parliament of the vast sum the nation has given for the best Paul Veronese in Venice —£14,000: I wonder what the nation meanwhile has given for its ball-dresses! Suppose we could see the London milliners' bills, simply for unnecessary breadths of slip and flounces, from April to July; I wonder whether £14,000 would cover *them*. But the breadths of slip and flounces are by this time as much lost and vanished as last year's snow; only they have done less good: but the Paul Veronese will last for centuries, if we take care of it; and yet we grumble at the price given for the painting, while no one grumbles at the price of pride.

Time does not permit me to go into any farther illustration of the various modes in which we build our statue out of snow, and waste our labor on things that vanish.

Things which are a mere luxury to one person are a means of intellectual occupation to another. Flowers in a London ball-room are a luxury; in a botanical garden, a delight of the intellect; and in their native fields, both; while the most noble works of art are continually made material of vulgar luxury or of criminal pride; but, when rightly used, property of this class is the only kind which deserves the name of *real* property; it is the only kind which a man can truly be said to "possess." What a man eats, or drinks, or wears, so long as it is only what is needful for life, can no more be thought of as his possession than the air he breathes. The air is as needful to him as the food; but we do not talk of a man's wealth of air, and what food or clothing a man possesses more than he himself requires, must be for others to use (and, to him, therefore, not a real property in itself, but only a means of obtaining some real property in exchange for it). Whereas the things that give intellectual or emotional enjoyment may be accumulated and do not perish in using; but continually supply new pleasures and new powers of giving pleasures to

others. And these, therefore, are the only
things which can rightly be thought of as giving
" wealth " or " well being." Food conduces
only to " being," but these to " *well* being."
And there is not any broader general distinction
between lower and higher orders of men than
rests on their possession of this real property.
The human race may be properly divided by
zoologists into " men who have gardens, libraries,
or works of art; and who have none;" and the
former class will include all noble persons, except only a few who make the world their garden
or museum; while the people who have not, or,
which is the same thing, do not care for gardens
or libraries, but care for nothing but money or
luxuries, will include none but ignoble persons:
only it is necessary to understand that I mean
by the term " garden " as much the Carthusian's
plot of ground fifteen feet square between his
monastery buttresses, as I do the grounds of
Chatsworth or Kew; and I mean by the term
" art " as much the old sailor's print of the Are-
thusa bearing up to engage the Belle Poule, as
I do Raphael's " Disputa," and even rather
more; for when abundant, beautiful possessions
of this kind are almost always associated with
vulgar luxury, and become then anything but
indicative of noble character in their possessors.
The ideal of human life is a union of Spartan

simplicity of manners with Athenian sensibility and imagination, but in actual results, we are continually mistaking ignorance for simplicity, and sensuality for refinement.

In general, pride is at the bottom of all great mistakes. All the other passions do occasional good, but wherever pride puts in *its* word, everything goes wrong, and what it might be desirable to do quietly and innocently, it is morally dangerous to do proudly.

To be content in utter darkness and ignorance is indeed unmanly, and therefore we think that to love light and seek knowledge must always be right. Yet wherever *pride* has any share in the work, even knowledge and light may be ill pursued. Knowledge is good, and light is good, yet man perished in seeking knowledge, and moths perished in seeking light; and if we, who are crushed before the moth, will not accept such mystery as is needful for us, we shall perish in like manner. But, accepted in humbleness, it instantly becomes an element of pleasure; and I think that every rightly constituted mind ought to rejoice, not so much in knowing anytihng clearly, as in feeling that there is infinitely more which it cannot know. None but proud or weak men would mourn over this, for we may always know more if we choose, by working on; but the pleasure is, I think, to humble people, in knowing that the journey is endless, the treasure inexhaustible,—watching the cloud still march before them with its summitless pillar, and being sure that, to the end of time and to the length of eternity, the mysteries of its infinity will still open farther and farther, their dimness being the sign and necessary adjunct of their inexhaustibleness. I know there are an evil mystery and a deathful dimness,—the mystery of the great Babylon—the dimness of the sealed eye and soul; but do not let us confuse these with the glorious mystery of the things which the angels " desire to look into," or with the dimness which, even before the clear eye and open soul, still rests on sealed pages of the eternal volume.

The ardor and abstraction of the spiritual life are to be honored in themselves, though the one may be misguided and the other deceived ; and the deserts of Osma, Assisi, and Monte Viso are still to be thanked for the zeal they gave, or guarded, whether we find it in St. Francis and St. Dominic, or in those whom God's hand hid from them in the clefts of the rocks.

We refine and explain ourselves into dim and distant suspicion of an inactive God, inhabiting

inconceivable places, and fading into the multitudinous formalisms of the laws of Nature.

All errors of this kind—and in the present
day we are in constant and grievous danger of
falling into them—arise from the originally mistaken idea that man can, " by searching, find out
God—find out the Almighty to perfection ;"
that is to say, by help of courses of reasoning
and accumulations of science, apprehend the
nature of the Deity in a more exalted and more
accurate manner than in a state of comparative
ignorance ; whereas it is clearly necessary, from
the beginning to the end of time, that God's way
of revealing himself to his creatures should be
a *simple* way, which *all* those creatures may
understand. Whether taught or untaught,
whether of mean capacity or enlarged, it is necessary that communion with their Creator should
be possible to all ; and the admission to such
communion must be rested, not on their having
a knowledge of astronomy, but on their having a
human soul. In order to render this communion
possible, the Deity has stooped from his throne,
and has not only, in the person of the Son, taken
upon him the veil of our human *flesh*, but, in
the person of the Father, taken upon him the
veil of our Human *thoughts*, and permitted us,
by his own spoken authority, to conceive him
simply and clearly as a loving Father and Friend;

—a being to be walked with and reasoned with; to be moved by our entreaties, angered by our rebellion, alienated by our coldness, pleased by our love, and glorified by our labor ; and, finally, to be beheld in immediate and active presence in all the powers and changes of creation. This conception of God, which is the child's, is evidently the only one which can be universal, and therefore the only one which *for us* can be true. The moment that, in our pride of heart, we refuse to accept the condescension of the Almighty, and desire him, instead of stooping to hold our hands, to rise up before us into his glory,—we hoping that by standing on a grain of dust or two of human knowledge higher than our fellows, we may behold the Creator as he rises,—God takes us at our word ; he rises, into his own invisible and inconceivable majesty ; he goes forth upon the ways which are not our ways, and retires into the thoughts which are not our thoughts ; and we are left alone. And presently we say in our vain hearts, "There is no God."

It may be proved, with much certainty, that God intends no man to live in this world without working : but it seems to me no less evident that he intends every man to be happy in his work. It is written, "in the sweat of thy brow,"

but it was never written, " in the breaking of
thine heart," thou shalt eat bread : and I find
that, as on the one hand, infinite misery is
caused by idle people, who both fail in doing
what was appointed for them to do, and set in
motion various springs of mischief in matters in
which they should have had no concern, so on
the other hand, no small misery is caused by
over-worked and unhappy people, in the dark
views which they necessarily take up themselves,
and force upon others, of work itself. Were it
not so, I believe the fact of their being unhappy
is in itself a violation of divine law, and a sign
of some kind of folly or sin in their way of life.
Now in order that people may be happy in their
work, these three things are needed : They must
be fit for it : They must not do too much of it :
and they must have a sense of success in it—not
a doubtful sense, such as needs some testimony
of other people for its confirmation, but a sure
sense, or rather knowledge, that so much work
has been done well, and fruitfully done, whatever the world may say or think about it. So
that in order that a man may be happy, it is
necessary that he should not only be capable of
his work, but a good judge of his work.

The first thing then that he has to do, if un-
happily his parents or masters have not done it
for him, is to find out what he is fit for. In

which inquiry a man may be very safely guided
by his likings, if he be not also guided by his
pride. People usually reason in some such
fashion as this : "I don't seem quite fit for a
head-manager in the firm of ——— & Co., therefore, in all probability, I am fit to be Chancellor
of the Exchequer." Whereas, they ought rather
to reason thus : "I don't seem quite fit to be
head-manager in the firm of ——— & Co., but I
dare say I might do something in a small green-
grocery business ; I used to be a good judge of
pease ;" that is to say, always trying lower
instead of trying higher, until they find bottom:
once well set on the ground, a man may build up
by degrees, safely, instead of disturbing every
one in his neighborhood by perpetual catastrophes. But this kind of humility is rendered especially difficult in these days, by the contume-
ly thrown on men in humble employments.
The very removal of the massy bars which once
separated one class of society from another, has
rendered it tenfold more shameful in foolish
people's, i.e. in most people's eyes, to remain in
the lower grades of it, than ever it was before.
When a man born of an artisan was looked
upon as an entirely different species of animal
from a man born of a noble, it made him no
more uncomfortable or ashamed to remain that
different species of animal, than it makes a horse

ashamed to remain a horse, and not to become
a giraffe.   But now that a man may make money,
and rise in the world, and associate himself, un-
reproached, with people once far above him, not
only is the natural discontentedness of humanity
developed to an unheard-of extent, whatever a
man's position, but it becomes a veritable shame
to him to remain in the state he was born in,
and everybody thinks it his *duty* to try to be a
" gentleman."   Persons who have any influence
in the management of public institutions for
charitable education know how common this
feeling has become.   Hardly a day passes but
they receive letters from mothers who want all
their six or eight sons to go to college, and make
the grand tour in the long vacation, and who
think there is something wrong in the foundations of society, because this is not possible.
Out of every ten letters of this kind, nine will
allege, as the reason of the writer's importunity,
their desire to keep their families in such and
such a " station of life."   There is no real desire
for the safety, the discipline, or the moral good
of the children, only a panic horror of the inex-
pressibly pitiable calamity of their living a ledge
or two lower on the molehill of the world—a
calamity to be averted at any cost whatever, of
struggle, anxiety, and shortening of life itself.   I
do not believe that any greater good could be

achieved for the country, than the change in public feeling on this head, which might be brought about by a few benevolent men, undeniably in the class of "gentlemen," who would, on principle, enter into some of our commonest trades, and make them honorable; showing that it was possible for a man to retain his dignity, and remain, in the best sense, a gentleman, though part of his time was every day occupied in manual labor, or even in serving customers over a counter. I do not in the least see why courtesy, and gravity, and sympathy with the feelings of others, and courage, and truth, and piety, and what else goes to make up a gentleman's character, should not be found behind a counter as well as elsewhere, if they were demanded, or even hoped for, there.

Let us suppose, then, that the man's way of life and manner of work have been discreetly chosen; then the next thing to be required is, that he do not overwork himself therein. I am not going to say anything here about the various errors in our systems of society and commerce, which appear (I am not sure if they ever do more than appear) to force us to overwork ourselves merely that we may live; nor about the still more fruitful cause of unhealthy toil—the incapability, in many men, of being content with the little that is indeed necessary to their happiness.

I have only a word or two to say about one special cause of over-work—the ambitious desire of
doing great or clever things, and the hope of accomplishing them by immense efforts ; hope as
vain as it is pernicious ; not only making men
overwork themselves, but rendering all the work
they do unwholesome to them. I say it is a vain
hope, and let the reader be assured of this (it is
a truth all-important to the best interests of humanity). *No great intellectual thing was ever
done by great effort;* a great thing can only be
done by a great man, and he does it *without* effort. Nothing is, at present, less understood by
us than this—nothing is more necessary to be
understood. Let me try to say it as clearly, and
explain it as fully as I may.

I have said no great *intellectual* thing : for I do
not mean the assertion to extend to things moral.
On the contrary, it seems to me that just because
we are intended, as long as we live, to be in a
state of intense moral effort, we are *not* intended
to be in intense physical or intellectual effort.
Our full energies are to be given to the soul's
work—to the great fight with the Dragon—the
taking the kingdom of heaven by force. But the
body's work and head's work are to be done
quietly, and comparatively without effort.
Neither limbs nor brain are ever to be strained
to their utmost ; that is not the way in which the

greatest quantity of work is to be got out of them : they are never to be worked furiously, but with tranquillity and constancy. We are to follow the plough from sunrise to sunset, but not to pull in race-boats at the twilight : we shall get no fruit of that kind of work, only disease of the heart.

How many pangs would be spared to thousands, if this great truth and law were but once sincerely, humbly understood,—that if a great thing can be done at all, it can be done easily ; that, when it is needed to be done, there is perhaps only one man in the world who can do it ; but *he* can do it without any trouble—without more trouble, that is, than it costs small people to do small things ; nay, perhaps, with less. And yet what truth lies more openly on the surface of all human phenomena ? Is not the evidence of Ease on the very front of all the greatest works in existence ? Do they not say plainly to us, not, " there has been a great *effort* here," but, " there has been a great *power* here "? It is not the weariness of mortality, but the strength of divinity, which we have to recognise in all mighty things ; and that is just what we now *never* recognise, but think that we are to do great things, by help of iron bars and perspiration,—alas ! we shall do nothing that way but lose some pounds of our own weight.

Yet, let me not be misunderstood, nor this great truth be supposed anywise resolvable into the favorite dogma of young men, that they need not work if they had genius. The fact is that a man of genius is always far more ready to work than other people, and get so much more good from the work that he does, and is often so little conscious of the inherent divinity in himself, that he is very apt to ascribe all his capacity to his work, and to tell those who ask how he came to be what he is : " If I *am* anything, which I much doubt, I made myself so merely by labor." This was Newton's way of talking, and I suppose it would be the general tone of men whose genius had been devoted to the physical sciences. Genius in the Arts must commonly be more self-conscious, but in whatever field, it will always be distinguished by its perpetual, steady, well directed, happy, and faithful labor in accumulating and disciplining its powers, as well as by its gigantic, incommunicable facility in exercising them. Therefore, literally, it is no man's business whether he has genius or not : work he must, whatever he is, but quietly and steadily ; and the natural and unforced results of such work will be always the things that God meant him to do, and will be his best. No agonies nor heart-rendings will enable him to do any better. If he be a great man, they will be great things ; if a small man, small things ; but always, if thus peacefully done, good and right ; always, if restlessly and ambitiously done, false, hollow, and despicable.

Then the third thing needed was, I said, that a man should be a good judge of his work ; and this chiefly that he may not be dependent upon popular opinion for the manner of doing it, but also that he may have the just encouragement of the sense of progress, and an honest conscious-ness of victory : how else can he become

> " That awful independent on to-morrow,
> Whose yesterdays look backwards with a smile " ?

I am persuaded that the real nourishment and help of such a feeling as this is nearly unknown to half the workmen of the present day. For whatever appearance of self-complacency there may be in their outward bearing, it is visible enough, by their feverish jealousy of each other, how little confidence they have in the sterling value of their several doings. Conceit may puff a man up, but never prop him up ; and there is too visible distress and hopelessness in men's as-pects to admit of the supposition that they have any stable support of faith in themselves.

I have stated these principles generally, be-cause there is no branch of labor to which they do not apply : But there is one in which our ig-

norance or forgetfulness of them has caused an
incalculable amount of suffering : and I would
endeavor now to reconsider them with especial
reference to it,—the branch of the Arts.

In general, the men who are employed in the
Arts have freely chosen their profession, and
suppose themselves to have special faculty for it;
yet, as a body, they are not happy men. For
which this seems to me the reason, that they are
expected, and themselves expect, to make their
bread *by being clever*—not by steady or quiet
work; and are, therefore, for the most part, trying to be clever, and so living in an utterly false
state of mind and action.

This is the case, to the same extent, in no
other profession or employment. A lawyer
may indeed suspect that, unless he has more wit
than those around him, he is not likely to advance in his profession; but he will not be always thinking how he is to display his wit. He
will generally understand, early in his career,
that wit must be left to take care of itself, and
that it is hard knowledge of law and vigorous
examination and collation of the facts of every
case entrusted to him, which his clients will
mainly demand: this it is which he has to be paid
for; and this is healthy and measurable labor.
payable by the hour. If he happen to have
keen natural perception and quick wit, these will

come into play in their due time and place, but he will not think of them as his chief power; and if he have them not, he may still hope that industry and conscientiousness may enable him to rise in his profession without them. Again in the case of clergymen: that they are sorely tempted to display their eloquence or wit, none who know their own hearts will deny, but then they *know* this to *be* a temptation: they never would suppose that cleverness was all that was to be expected from them, or would sit down deliberately to write a clever sermon: even the dullest or vainest of them would throw some veil over their vanity, and pretend to some profitableness of purpose in what they did. They would not openly ask of their hearers—Did you think my sermon ingenious, or my language poetical? They would early understand that they were not paid for being ingenious, nor called to be so, but to preach truth; that if they happened to possess wit, eloquence, or originality, these would appear and be of service in due time, but were not to be continually sought after or exhibited: and if it should happen that they had them not, they might still be serviceable pastors without them.

Not so with the unhappy artist. No one expects any honest or useful work of him; but every one expects him to be ingenious. Origi-

nality, dexterity, invention, imagination, every
thing is asked of him except what alone is to be
had for asking—honesty and sound work, and
the due discharge of his function as a painter.
What function? asks the reader in some surprise.
He may well ask; for I suppose few painters have
any idea what their function is, or even that they
have any at all.

And yet surely it is not so difficult to discover.
The faculties, which when a man finds in himself, he resolves to be a painter, are, I suppose,
intenseness of observation and facility of imitation. The man is created an observer and an imitator; and his function is to convey knowledge
to his fellow-men, of such things as cannot be
taught otherwise than ocularly. For a long time
this function remained a religious one: it was to
impress upon the popular mind the reality of
the objects of faith, and the truth of the histories of Scripture, by giving visible form to both.
That function has now passed away, and none
has as yet taken its place. The painter has no
profession, no purpose. He is an idler on the
earth, chasing the shadows of his own fancies.

But he was never meant to be this.

I do not know anything more ludicrous among
the self-deceptions of well-meaning people than
their notion of patriotism, as requiring them to

limit their efforts to the good of their own country;—the notion that charity is a geographical
virtue, and that what it is holy and righteous to
do for people on one bank of a river, it is quite
improper and unnatural to do for people on the
other. It will be a wonderful thing, some day
or other, for the Christian world to remember,
that it went on thinking for two thousand years
that neighbors were neighbors at Jerusalem, but
not at Jericho; a wonderful thing for us English
to reflect, in after-years, how long it was before
we could shake hands with anybody across the
shallow salt wash, which the very chalk-dust of
its two shores whitens from Folkestone to Am-
bleteuse.

It would be well if, instead of preaching continually about the doctrine of faith and good
works, our clergymen would simply explain to
their people a little what good works mean.
There is not a chapter in all the book we profess to believe more specially and directly written
for England, than the second of Habakkuk, and
I never in all my life heard one of its practical
texts preached from. I suppose the clergymen
are all afraid, and know that their flocks, while
they will sit quite politely to hear syllogisms out
of the epistle to the Romans, would get restive
directly if they ever pressed a practical text

home to them.   But we should have no mercan-
tile catastrophes, and no distressful pauperism,
if we only read often, and took to heart, those
plain words: "Yea, also, because he is a proud
man, neither keepeth at home, who enlargeth his
desire as hell, and cannot be satisfied,—Shall
not all these take up a parable against him, and
a taunting proverb against him, and say, 'Woe
to him that increaseth that which is not his: and
to him that *ladeth himself with thick clay.*'"
(What a glorious history, in one metaphor, of
the life of a man greedy of fortune.) "Woe to
him that coveteth an evil covetousness that he
may set his nest on high. Woe to him that
buildeth a town with blood, and stablisheth a
city by iniquity. Behold, is it not of the Lord
of Hosts that the people shall labor in the very
fire, and the people shall weary themselves for
very vanity?"

"She riseth while it is yet night, and giveth
meat to her household, and a portion to her
maidens. She maketh herself coverings of tap-
estry, her clothing is silk and purple. Strength
and honor are in her clothing, and she shall rejoice in time to come."

Now, you will observe that in this description
of the perfect economist, or mistress of a household, there is a studied expression of the bal-

anced division of her care between the two great
objects of utility and splendor; in her right
hand, food and flax, for life and clothing; in her
left hand, the purple and the needle-work, for
honor and for beauty.   All perfect housewifery
or national economy is known by these two divisions; wherever either is wanting, the economy
is imperfect.   If the motive of pomp prevails, and
the care of the national economist is directed
only to the accumulation of gold, and of pictures,
and of silk and marble, you know at once that
the time must soon come when all these treasures
shall be scattered and blasted in national ruin.
If, on the contrary, the element of utility prevails, and the nation disdains to occupy itself in
any wise with the arts of beauty or delight, not
only a certain quantity of its energy calculated
for exercise in those arts alone must be entirely
wasted, which is bad economy, but also the passions connected with the utilities of property
become morbidly strong, and a mean lust of accumulation, merely for the sake of accumulation,
or even of labor, merely for the sake of labor,
will banish at least the serenity and the morality of life, as completely, and perhaps more
ignobly, than even the lavishness of pride, and
the lightness of pleasure.   And similarly, and
much more visibly, in private and household
economy, you may judge always of its perfect-

ness by its fair balance between the use and the pleasure of its possessions.

That modern science, with all its additions to the comforts of life, and to the fields of rational contemplation, has placed the existing races of mankind on a higher platform than preceded them, none can doubt for an instant; and I believe the position in which we find ourselves is somewhat analogous to that of thoughtful and laborious youth succeeding a restless and heedless infancy. Not long ago, it was said to me by one of the masters of modern sciences: " When men invented the locomotive, the child was learning to go; when they invented the telegraph, it was learning to speak." He looked forward to the manhood of mankind, as assuredly the nobler in proportion to the slowness of its development. What might not be expected from the prime and middle strength of the order of existence whose infancy had lasted six thousand years? And indeed, I think this the truest, as well as the most cheering, view that we can take of the world's history. Little progress has been made as yet. Base war, lying policy, thoughtless cruelty, senseless improvidence,—all things which, in nations, are analogous to the petulance, cunning, impatience, and carelessness of infancy, —have been, up to this hour, as characteristic of mankind as they were in the earliest periods; so that we must either be driven to doubt of human progress at all, or look upon it as in its very earliest stage. Whether the opportunity is to be permitted us to redeem the hours that we have lost; whether He in whose sight a thousand years are as one day, has appointed us to be tried by the continued possession of the strange powers with which he has lately endowed us; or whether the period of childhood and of probation are to cease together, and the youth of mankind is to be one which shall prevail over death, and bloom for ever in the midst of a new heaven and a new earth, are questions with which we have no concern. It is indeed right that we should look for, and hasten, so far as in us lies, the coming of the Day of God; but not that we should check any human efforts by anticipations of its approach. We shall hasten it best by endeavoring to work out the tasks that are appointed for us here; and, therefore, reasoning as if the world were to continue under its existing dispensation, and the powers which have just been granted to us were to be continued through myriads of future ages.

In the early ages of Christianity, there was little care taken to analyse character. One momentous question was heard over the whole

world; "Dost thou believe in the Lord with all
thine heart?" There was but one division
among men,—the great unatoneable division between the disciple and adversary. The love of
Christ was all, and in all; and in proportion to
the nearness of their memory of his person and
teaching, men understood the infinity of the requirements of the moral law, and the manner in
which it alone could be fulfilled. The early
Christians felt that virtue, like sin, was a subtle
universal thing, entering into every act and
thought, appearing outwardly in ten thousand
diverse ways, diverse according to the separate
framework of every heart in which it dwelt; but
one and the same always in its proceeding from
the love of God, as sin is one and the same in
proceeding from hatred of God. And in their
pure, early, and practical piety they saw that
there was no need for codes of morality, or
systems of metaphysics. Their virtue comprehended everything, entered into everything; it
was too vast and too spiritual to be defined; but
there was no need of its definition. For through
faith, working by love, they knew that all human
excellence would be developed in due order;
but that, without faith, neither reason could
define, nor effort reach, the lowest phase of
Christian virtue. And therefore, when any of
the Apostles have occasion to describe or enu-

merate any forms of vice or virtue by name, there is no attempt at system in their words. They use them hurriedly and energetically, heaping the thoughts one upon another, in order as far as possible to fill the reader's mind with a sense of infinity both of crime and of righteousness. Hear St. Paul describe sin: "Being filled with all unrighteousness, fornication, wickedness, covetousness, maliciousness; full of envy, murder, debate, deceit, malignity, whisperers, backbiters, haters of God, despiteful, proud, boasters, inventors of evil things, disobedient to parents, without understanding, covenant breakers, without natural affection, implacable, unmerciful." There is evidently here an intense feeling of the universality of sin; and in order to express it, the Apostle hurries his words confusedly together, little caring about their order, as knowing all the vices to be indissolubly connected one with another. It would be utterly vain to endeavor to arrange his expressions as if they had been intended for the ground of any system, or to give any philosophical definition of the vices. So also hear him speaking of virtue: "Rejoice in the Lord. Let your moderation be known unto all men. Be careful for nothing, but in everything let your requests be made known unto God; and whatsoever things are honest, whatsoever things are just, whatsoever things are

pure, whatsoever things are lovely, whatsoever
things are of good report, if there be any virtue,
and if there be any praise, think on these things."
Observe, he gives up all attempt at definition,
he leaves the definition to every man's heart,
though he writes so as to mark the overflowing
fulness of his own vision of virtue. And so it is
in all writings of the Apostles; their manner
of exhortation, and the kind of conduct they
press, vary according to the persons they address, and the feeling of the moment at which
they write, and never show any attempt at logical precision. And, although the words of
their Master are not thus irregularly uttered, but
are weighed like fine gold, yet, even in his teaching, there is no detailed or organized system of
morality; but the command only of that faith
and love which were to embrace the whole being
of man; "On these two commandments hang all
the law and the prophets." Here and there an
incidental warning against this or that more
dangerous form of vice or error, "Take heed and
beware of covetousness," "Beware of the leaven
of the Pharisees," here and there a plain example of the meaning of Christian love, as in
the parables of the Samaritan and the Prodigal,
and his own perpetual example: these were the
elements of Christ's constant teachings; for the
Beatitudes, which are the only approximation to

anything like a systematic statement, belong to different conditions and characters of individual men, not to abstract virtues. And all early Christians taught in the same manner. They never cared to expound the nature of this or that virtue; for they knew that the believer who had Christ, had all. Did he need fortitude? Christ was his rock: Equity? Christ was his righteousness: Holiness? Christ was his sanctification: Liberty? Christ was his redemption: Temperance? Christ was his ruler: Wisdom? Christ was his light: Truthfulness? Christ was the truth: Charity? Christ was love.

Now, exactly in proportion as the Christian religion became less vital, and as the various corruptions which time and Satan brought into it were able to manifest themselves, the person and offices of Christ were less dwelt upon, and the virtues of Christians more. The Life of the Believer became in some degree separated from the Life of Christ; and his virtue, instead of being a stream flowing forth from the throne of God, and descending upon the earth, began to be regarded by him as a pyramid upon earth, which he had to build up, step by step, that from the top of it he might reach the Heavens.

I understand not the most dangerous, because most attractive form of modern infidelity, which

pretending to exalt the beneficence of the Deity,
degrades it into a reckless infinitude of mercy,
and blind obliteration of the work of sin; and
which does this chiefly by dwelling on the manifold appearances of God's kindness on the face
of creation. Such kindness is indeed everywhere and always visible; but not alone. Wrath
and threatening are invariably mingled with the
love, and in the utmost solitudes of nature, the
existence of Hell seems to me as legibly declared
by a thousand spiritual utterances, as that of
Heaven. It is well for us to dwell with thankfulness on the unfolding of the flower, and the
falling of the dew, and the sleep of the green
fields in the sunshine, but the blasted trunk, the
barren rock, the moaning of the bleak winds, the
roar of the black, perilous, merciless whirlpools
of the mountain streams, the solemn solitudes of
moors and seas, the continual fading of all beauty
into darkness, and of all strength into dust, have
these no language for us ? We may seek to escape
their teachings by reasonings touching the good
which is wrought out of all evil ; but it is vain
sophistry. The good succeeds to the evil as day
succeeds the night, but so also the evil to the
good. Gerizim and Ebal, birth and death, light
and darkness, heaven and hell, divide the existence of man and his Futurity.

And because the thoughts of the choice we

have to make between these two, ought to rule us continually, not so much in our own actions (for these should, for the most part, be governed by settled habit and principle) as in our manner of regarding the lives of other men, and our own responsibilities with respect to them; therefore, it seems to me that the healthiest state into which the human mind can be brought is that which is capable of the greatest love, and the greatest awe.

When the sermon is good we need not much concern ourselves about the form of the pulpit. But sermons cannot always be good; and I believe that the temper in which the congregation set themselves to listen may be in some degree modified by their perception of fitness or unfitness, impressiveness or vulgarity, in the disposition of the place appointed for the speaker,— not to the same degree, but somewhat in the same way, that they may be influenced by his own gestures or expression, irrespective of the sense of what he says. I believe therefore, in the first place, that pulpits ought never to be highly decorated; the speaker is apt to look mean or diminutive if the pulpit is either on a very large scale or covered with splendid ornament, and if the interest of the sermon should flag, the mind is instantly tempted to wander

I have observed that in almost all cathedrals when the pulpits are peculiarly magnificent, sermons are not often preached from them; but rather, and especially if for any important purpose, from some temporary erection in other parts of the building: and though this may often be done because the architect has consulted the effect upon the eye more than the convenience of the ear in the placing of his larger pulpit, I think it also proceeds in some measure from a natural dislike in the preacher to match himself with the magnificence of the rostrum, lest the sermon should not be thought worthy of the place. Yet, this will rather hold of the colossal sculptures, and pyramids of fantastic tracery which encumber the pulpits of Flemish and German churches, than of the delicate mosaics and ivory-like carving of the Romanesque basilicas, for when the form is kept simple, *much* loveliness of color and costliness of work may be introduced, and yet the speaker not be thrown into the shade by them.

But, in the second place, whatever ornaments we admit ought clearly to be of a chaste, grave, and noble kind; and what furniture we employ, evidently more for the honoring of God's word than for the ease of the preacher. For there are two ways of regarding a sermon, either as a human composition, or a Divine message. If we look upon it entirely as the first, and require our clergymen to finish it with their utmost care and learning, for our better delight whether of ear or intellect, we shall necessarily be led to expect much formality and stateliness in its delivery, and to think that all is not well if the pulpit have not a golden fringe round it, and a goodly cushion in front of it, and if the sermon be not fairly written in a black book, to be smoothed upon the cushion in a majestic manner before beginning; all this we shall duly come to expect: but we shall at the same time consider the treatise thus prepared as something to which it is our duty to listen without restlessness for half an hour or three quarters, but which, when that duty has been decorously performed, we may dismiss from our minds in happy confidence of being provided with another when next it shall be necessary. But if once we begin to regard the preacher, whatever his faults, as a man sent with a message to us, which it is a matter of life or death whether we hear or refuse; if we look upon him as set in charge over many spirits in danger of ruin, and having allowed to him but an hour or two in the seven days to speak to them; if we make some endeavor to conceive how precious these hours ought to be to him, a small vantage on the side of God after his flock have been exposed for six days together

to the full weight of the world's temptation, and
he has been forced to watch the thorn and the
thistle springing in their hearts, and to see what
wheat had been scattered there snatched from
the wayside by this wild bird and the other, and
at last, when breathless and weary with the
week's labor they give him this interval of imperfect and languid hearing, he has but thirty
minutes to get at the separate hearts of a thousand men, to convince them of all their weaknesses, to shame them for all their sins, to warn
them of all their dangers, to try by this way and
that to stir the hard fastenings of those doors
where the Master himself has stood and knocked
yet none opened, and to call at the openings of
those dark streets where Wisdom herself hath
stretched forth her hands and no man regarded,
—thirty minutes to raise the dead in,—let us but
once understand and feel this, and we shall look
with changed eyes upon that frippery of gay furniture about the place from which the message
of judgment must be delivered, which either
breathes upon the dry bones that they may live,
or, if ineffectual, remains recorded in condemna-
tion, perhaps against the utterer and listener
alike, but assuredly against one of them. We
shall not so easily bear with the silk and gold
upon the seat of judgment, nor with ornament
of oratory in the mouth of the messenger; we

shall wish that his words may be simple, even
when they are sweetest, and the place from
which he speaks like a marble rock in the desert,
about which the people have gathered in their
thirst.

———◆———

MODERN EDUCATION.

By a large body of the people of England and
of Europe a man is called educated if he can
write Latin verses and construe a Greek chorus.
By some few more enlightened persons it is confessed that the construction of hexameters is
not in itself an important end of human existence; but they say, that the general discipline
which a course of classical reading gives to the
intellectual powers, is the final object of our
scholastical institutions.

But it seems to me, there is no small error
even in this last and more philosophical theory.
I believe, that what it is most honorable to
know, it is also most profitable to learn; and
that the science which it is the highest power
to possess, it is also the best exercise to acquire.

And if this be so, the question as to what
should be the material of education, becomes
singularly simplified. It might be matter of dis-

pute what processes have the greatest effect in developing the intellect; but it can hardly be disputed what facts it is most advisable that a man entering into life should accurately know.

I believe, in brief, that he ought to know three things:

First. Where he is.

Secondly. Where he is going.

Thirdly. What he had best do under those circumstances.

First. Where he is.—That is to say, what sort of a world he has got into; how large it is; what kind of creatures live in it, and how; what it is made of, and what may be made of it.

Secondly. Where he is going.—That is to say, what chances or reports there are of any other world besides this; what seems to be the nature of that other world; and whether, for information respecting it, he had better consult the Bible, Koran, or Council of Trent.

Thirdly. What he had best do under those circumstances.—That is to say, what kind of faculties he possesses; what are the present state and wants of mankind; what is his place in society; and what are the readiest means in his power of attaining happiness and diffusing it. The man who knows these things, and who has had his will so subdued in the learning them, that he is ready to do what he knows he ought,

I should call educated; and the man who knows them not, uneducated, though he could talk all the tongues of Babel.

Our present European system of so-called education ignores, or despises, not one, nor the other, but all the three, of these great branches of human knowledge.

First: It despises Natural History.—Until within the last year or two, the instruction in the physical sciences given at Oxford consisted of a course of twelve or fourteen lectures on the Elements of Mechanics or Pneumatics, and permission to ride out to Shotover with the Professor of Geology. I do not know the specialties of the system pursued in the academies of the Continent; but their practical result is, that unless a man's natural instincts urge him to the pursuit of the physical sciences too strongly to be resisted, he enters into life utterly ignorant of them. I cannot, within my present limits, even so much as count the various directions in which this ignorance does evil. But the main mischief of it is, that it leaves the greater number of men without the natural food which God intended for their intellects. For one man who is fitted for the study of words, fifty are fitted for the study of things, and were intended to have a perpetual, simple, and religious delight in watching the processes, or admiring the creatures, of the natural universe.   Deprived of this source of pleasure, nothing is left to them but ambition or dissipation; and the vices of the upper classes of Europe are, I believe, chiefly to be attributed to this single cause.

Secondly: It despises Religion.—I do not say it despises "Theology," that is to say, *talk* about God.   But it despises "Religion;" that is to say, the "binding" or training to God's service. There is much talk and much teaching in all our academies, of which the effect is not to bind, but to loosen, the elements of religious faith. Of the ten or twelve young men who, at Oxford, were my especial friends, who sat with me under the same lectures on Divinity, or were punished with me for missing lecture by being sent to evening prayers, four are now zealous Roman- ists, a large average out of twelve; and while thus our own universities profess to teach Prot- estantism, and do not, the universities on the Continent profess to teach Romanism, and do not,—sending forth only rebels and infidels. During long residence on the Continent, I do not remember meeting with above two or three young men, who either believed in revelation, or had the grace to hesitate in the assertion of their infidelity.

Whence, it seems to me, we may gather one of two things; either that there is nothing in any European form of religion so reasonable or ascertained, as that it can be taught securely to our youth, or fastened in their minds by any rivets of proof which they shall not be able to loosen the moment they begin to think; or else, that no means are taken to train them in such demonstrable creeds.

It seems to me the duty of a rational nation to ascertain (and to be at some pains in the matter) which of these suppositions is true; and, if indeed no proof can be given of any supernatural fact, or Divine doctrine, stronger than a youth just out of his teens can overthrow in the first stirrings of serious thought, to confess this boldly; to get rid of the expense of an Establishment, and the hypocrisy of a Liturgy; to exhibit its cathedrals as curious memorials of a bygone superstition, and, abandoning all thoughts of the next world, to set itself to make the best it can of this.

But if, on the other hand, there does exist any evidence by which the probability of certain religious facts may be shown, as clearly, even, as the probabilities of things not absolutely ascertained in astronomical or geological science, let this evidence be set before all our youth so distinctly, and the facts for which it appears inculcated upon them so steadily, that although it may be possible for the evil conduct

of after life to efface, or for its earnest and pro-
tracted meditation to modify, the impressions
of early years, it may not be possible for our
young men, the instant they emerge from their
academies, to scatter themselves like a flock of
wild fowl risen out of a marsh, and drift away
on every irregular wind of heresy and apostasy.

Lastly. Our System of European education
despises politics.—That is to say, the science of
the relations and duties of men to each other.
One would imagine, indeed, by a glance at the
state of the world, that there was no such science.   And, indeed, it is one still in its infancy.

It implies, in its full sense, the knowledge of
the operations of the virtues and vices of men
upon themselves and society; the understanding
of the ranks and offices of their intellectual
and bodily powers in their various adaptations
to art, science, and industry; the understanding
of the proper offices of art, science, and labor
themselves, as well as of the foundations of ju-
risprudence, and broad principles of commerce;
all this being coupled with practical knowledge
of the present state and wants of mankind.

What, it will be said, and is all this to be taught
to schoolboys ? No; but the first elements of
it, all that are necessary to be known by an individual in order to his acting wisely in any station of life might be taught, not only to every

schoolboy, but to every peasant. The impossibility of equality among men; the good which
arises from their inequality; the compensating
circumstances in different states and fortunes;
the honorableness of every man who is worthily
filling his appointed place in society, however
humble; the proper relations of poor and rich,
governor and governed; the nature of wealth,
and mode of its circulation; the difference between productive and unproductive labor; the
relation of the products of the mind and hand;
the true value of works of the higher arts, and
the possible amount of their production; the
meaning of " Civilization," its advantages and
dangers; the meaning of the term " Refinement;" the possibilities of possessing refinement
in a low station, and of losing it in a high one;
and, above all, the significance of almost every
act of a man's daily life, in its ultimate operation upon himself and others;—all this might
be, and ought to be, taught to every boy in the
Kingdom, so completely, that it should be just
as impossible to introduce an absurd or licen-
tious doctrine among our adult population, as a
new version of the multiplication table. Nor
am I altogether without hope that some day it
may enter into the heads of the tutors of our
schools to try whether it is not as easy to make
an Eton's boy's mind as sensitive to falseness in

policy, as his ear is at present to falseness in prosody.

I know that this is much to hope. That English ministers of religion should ever come to desire rather to make a youth acquainted with the powers of Nature and of God, than with the powers of Greek particles; that they should ever think it more useful to show him how the great universe rolls upon its course in heaven, than how the syllables are fitted in a tragic metre; that they should hold it more advisable for him to be fixed in the principles of religion than in those of syntax; or, finally, that they should ever come to apprehend that a youth likely to go straight out of college into parliament, might not unadvisably know as much of the Peninsular as of the Peloponnesian War, and be as well acquainted with the state of Modern Italy as of old Etruria;—all this, however unreasonably, I do hope, and mean to work for. For though I have not yet abandoned all expectation of a better world than this, I believe this in which we live is not so good as it might be. I know there are many people who suppose French revolutions, Italian insurrections, Caffre wars, and such other scenic efforts of modern policy, to be among the normal conditions of humanity. I know there are many who think the atmosphere of rapine, rebellion, and misery which wraps the lower orders of Europe more closely every day, is as natural a phenomenon as a hot summer. But God forbid! There are ills which flesh is heir to and troubles to which man is born; but the troubles which he is born to are as sparks which fly upward, not as flames burning to the nethermost Hell. The poor we must have with us always, and sorrow is inseparable from any hour of life; but we may make their poverty such as shall inherit the earth, and the sorrow, such as shall be hallowed by the hand of the Comforter, with everlasting comfort. We can, if we will but shake off this lethargy and dreaming that is upon us, and take the pains to think and act like men, we can, I say, make kingdoms to be like well governed households, in which, indeed while no care or kindness can prevent occasional heartburnings, nor any foresight or piety anticipate all the vicissitudes of fortune, or avert every stroke of calamity, yet the unity of their affection and fellowship remains unbroken, and their distress is neither embittered by division, prolonged by imprudence, nor darkened by dishonor.

THE END.

END NOTES

1. Definition provided by www.dictionary.com
2. Ibid
3. Ibid
4. zombie.wikia.com
5. Ibid
6. Ibid
7. http://en.wikipedia.org/wiki/Zombie_%28fictional%29
8. http://en.wikipedia.org/wiki/Human_brain